Samuel French Acting Edition

The Emigrants

by Slawomir Mrozek

Translated by Henry Beissel

SAMUELFRENCH.COM   SAMUELFRENCH.CO.UK

Copyright © 1984 by Henry Beissel
All Rights Reserved

THE EMIGRANTS is fully protected under the copyright laws of the United States of America, the British Commonwealth, including Canada, and all other countries of the Copyright Union. All rights, including professional and amateur stage productions, recitation, lecturing, public reading, motion picture, radio broadcasting, television and the rights of translation into foreign languages are strictly reserved.

ISBN 978-0-573-64032-2

www.SamuelFrench.com
www.SamuelFrench.co.uk

FOR PRODUCTION ENQUIRIES

UNITED STATES AND CANADA
Info@SamuelFrench.com
1-866-598-8449

UNITED KINGDOM AND EUROPE
Plays@SamuelFrench.co.uk
020-7255-4302

Each title is subject to availability from Samuel French, depending upon country of performance. Please be aware that *THE EMIGRANTS* may not be licensed by Samuel French in your territory. Professional and amateur producers should contact the nearest Samuel French office or licensing partner to verify availability.

CAUTION: Professional and amateur producers are hereby warned that *THE EMIGRANTS* is subject to a licensing fee. Publication of this play(s) does not imply availability for performance. Both amateurs and professionals considering a production are strongly advised to apply to Samuel French before starting rehearsals, advertising, or booking a theatre. A licensing fee must be paid whether the title(s) is presented for charity or gain and whether or not admission is charged. Professional/Stock licensing fees are quoted upon application to Samuel French.

No one shall make any changes in this title(s) for the purpose of production. No part of this book may be reproduced, stored in a retrieval system, or transmitted in any form, by any means, now known or yet to be invented, including mechanical, electronic, photocopying, recording, videotaping, or otherwise, without the prior written permission of the publisher. No one shall upload this title(s), or part of this title(s), to any social media websites.

For all enquiries regarding motion picture, television, and other media rights, please contact Samuel French.

Please refer to page 86 for further copyright information.

The Emigrants

Gray, dirty walls with large blots and stains. A basement. A naked bulb hangs from the ceiling. The light is glaring. On the right wall at the back there is a door. (Note: right and left are always right and left as seen from the audience's point of view.) There is no window. Along the two walls on the right and left there are two iron bedsteads. Above the bed on the right there is a nail, from which hang a coat as well as a wooden coat rack.

There is an old sink or basin, mounted directly on top of a drain-pipe, against the back wall, about a quarter of the way from the left. The cracked enamel of the sink has turned yellow with age. The drain-pipe is covered with rust spots. Above the sink a bronze tap. Above the tap, a very ordinary shelf. Two toilet bags, one very cheap, the other more fancy. Above the shelf, a fairly large mirror of bad quality hangs from a nail. A towel hangs from a nail on either side of the sink. Near the back wall, a little further to the right, an old screen in a very dilapidated state. Also, there are all kinds of pipes of different sizes running along the back wall right through the whole room as well as electric cables.

Stage centre, directly under the bulb, a table covered with newspapers. On the table there are two dirty plates, two spoons, two plastic tumblers, two open cans of food, one empty beer bottle, and one box with tea-bags.

Cigarette butts. Two chairs on opposite sides of the table. On the chair on the right side, a pair of light grey trousers. Over the back of it, a tweed jacket and a silk tie. Under the chair, a pair of shoes. A man, badly shaven, in a dressing gown, is stretched out on the bed to the left. He is wearing socks and points his feet to the audience. He is a lean man in his thirties. His hair is thinning slightly. He wears glasses with dark plastic frames. He is reading.

On the bed on the right, a huge plush dog in vivid colours. A man is sitting on the chair on the right. He wears an old-fashioned black suit cut from a thick material, a little like the sort of suits worn on Sundays by the peasants of certain countries or certain regions. A white shirt, a tie in garish colours. His shoes are very pointed and carefully polished. The man is portly, built like a wrestler. He has enormous hands. His chubby face is clean shaven. Lots of hair, sideburns. He is sitting with this profile to the audience, looking at his partner stretched out on the bed. The two are about the same age.

For a few moments, the first (AA) reads, stretched out on the bed; the second (XX) remains seated watching him.

XX. It's me! (*AA doesn't react. Pause.*) I got back.

AA. (*without interrupting his reading*) One says: "I *am* back," not "I got back."

XX. (*scratching his calves*) Got a cigarette? (*Without interrupting his reading, AA reaches under his pillow and brings out a package of cigarettes which he holds out to XX, who gets up and hobbles over to the bed. He takes a cigarette. AA goes on reading. XX slips the cigarette into his pocket and takes a second one. After a moment's hesitation he takes a third cigarette after slipping the second into his pocket as well. He puts the third cigarette in his mouth.*) That's it. I've helped myself. (*AA continues to hold the package of cigarettes at arm's length without taking his eyes off his book. Pause.*)

THE EMIGRANTS

AA. Put them back . . . (*XX takes one cigarette out of his pocket and puts it back in the package. He turns around and walks away. AA still holds up his package of cigarettes, his arms outstretched, and goes on reading.*) Put them back . . .

XX. I put one back.

AA. You took three. (*XX takes the second cigarette from his pocket and puts it back in the package. AA, who goes on reading, slips the package under his pillow. XX goes back to the middle of the room. He takes a box of matches from his pocket, opens it, takes out a match and is about to strike it when he stops his movements and looks in the direction of AA. Seeing that he is still reading, XX puts the match back in its box and slips the box back in his pocket. He goes to the chair on which the tweed jacket hangs. He feels the pockets, finds a box of matches and takes it out. He lights his cigarette and slips the box of matches in his left pocket. XX seats himself in the same chair and in the same position as at the beginning. With obvious pleasure he inhales the smoke of his cigarette. He scratches the calves of his legs, unbuttons his shirt collar, undoes his tie, takes off his shoes. His socks are riddled with large holes. He blows on his shoes which shine, as though he were removing invisible specks of dust, then he puts them delicately by the side of his chair. He stretches his legs with satisfaction and wiggles his toes.*)

XX. I went to the bus terminal.

AA. (*without interrupting his reading*) So what?

XX. Nothing. Loads of people. (*pause*) I had a beer.

AA. (*incredulous*) You did?

XX. I'm telling you. (*pause*) Two beers. (*pause*) In the bar.

AA. Well!

XX. They got public phones.
AA. So what?
XX. Nothing. People telephone.
AA. Hmmm.
XX. I didn't use the phones. I said to myself: What's the point of calling anyone . . . So I just stood next to them.
AA. Good. (*pause*)
XX. There's newsstands too.
AA. Oh?
XX. They sell newspapers. But lots of other things as well.
AA. So what?
XX. Nothing. People were buying papers.
AA. Really?
XX. And they read them . . . I didn't read any. I said to myself: What's the point of reading a newspaper?
AA. Of course.
XX. So, I just stood next to the racks of papers. (*pause*) They've got wickets. (*Pause. AA doesn't react.*) I said, they've got wickets.
AA. What?
XX. For selling tickets.
AA. Tickets?
XX. People were buying tickets. (*AA whistles in admiration.*) I didn't buy one. I just stood next to the wickets.
AA. You were right.
XX. Then I said to myself: I'm gonna take a walk on the platform.
AA. Why?
XX. Because it's free. Back home you've got to buy a ticket to go on the platform, but here they let you pass for nothing. They're stupid.

THE EMIGRANTS

AA. (*distracted*) Who is?

XX. Them. —So I went on the platform.

AA. Aha. Then what?

XX. Nothing. A whole row of buses. And it was blowing.

AA. What was blowing?

XX. The wind. So I said to myself: I'm going back in. Just then there was an announcement over the loudspeaker. So I decided to stay. And I stayed. But the wine was cold. Just as I'm going to go back in what d'you think I see pull into the station?

AA. A bus.

XX. How did you know? (*pause*) That's right. A bus. International, the bus. It had six number plates and a big dog on the side. And me, I don't move. I just light a cigarette.

AA. Did someone offer you one?

XX. I had my own. Anyways, I don't move and I say to myself: Here, come here, my pet. . . , here. You're not going any further, this is the terminal. Come on! —And so the bus comes closer and closer till . . .

AA. . . . it came to a stop.

XX. How did you know? (*pause*) It came to a complete stop. So I said to myself: You see? I told you you wouldn't go any further . . .

AA. (*turning a page in his book*) And the bus?

XX. Nothing. It just stood there.

AA. Is that all?

XX. Right away people got off the bus. They got cold waiting for their luggage. Beautiful luggage: suitcases, bags . . . Me, I don't move. I just smoke very calmly. I said to myself: I'm gonna finish my cigarette and then I go. By this time they'd all gotten off. Just as I'm about to flick away my butt, there, right in front of me, a woman gets up in the bus. She's waiting inside, where it's warm. Not bad, eh?

AA. Interesting.

XX. Oh my God! She had hair down to here, she must've been an actress. So I said to myself: I'm gonna wait just a little longer till she's off. My butt was burning my fingers. I passed it from one hand to the other. And I said to myself: she's got to get off.

AA. And then?

XX. (*triumphant*) She got off.

AA. You were lucky. (*long pause*) Finished already? (*XX laughs.*) Why are you laughing? (*XX continues to laugh.*) What's so funny in all this?

XX. Well, I . . . followed her. (*For the first time AA looks up from his book at XX.*)

AA. You what?

XX. Well . . . (*He laughs.*)

AA. Stop laughing!

XX. You're just jealous . . . If you knew how she . . . and I . . .

AA. Where?

XX. In the washroom.

AA. What?

XX. Well, yes! In the Ladies Washroom. She went in first, then I . . . hop hop, unseen is unknown—two times! (*AA closes his book.*) She wanted more, but I didn't feel like it. (*AA takes off his glasses and puts them in the pocket of his dressing gown. He turns to lie on his side, supported on his elbow, and looks at XX*).

AA. And after that?

XX. Nothing.

AA. What do you mean *nothing?*

XX. Nothing. Like I told you, I didn't feel like it any more. Her, she wanted more, but I didn't feel like going on.

THE EMIGRANTS

AA. Alright. But afterwards?

XX. Afterwards? Oh well, I left.

AA. And she?

XX. She too, she left.

AA. You didn't get her address?

XX. No. She wanted to give it to me, but I said to myself: what for? . . . And then there's always the risk that I'd lose it . . .

AA. But she wanted you to take it, her address I mean.

XX. Yes, she insisted. (*pause*) An ambassador came to pick her up. I think it was her husband. In a big car with a little flag.

AA. Aha. (*He fetches his package of cigarettes, takes a cigarette, searches for matches in the pocket of his dressing gown, gets up, goes over to the chair to search the pockets of his jacket, but can't find any matches.*)

XX. A light? (*AA goes over to him; XX produces matches from the left-hand pocket of his jacket and gives him a light. AA picks a pair of trousers off the chair and throws them on the bed. He sits down and inhales deeply from his cigarette.*)

AA. You want to know what happened?

XX. I just told you.

AA. No, no. I mean do you want to know what really happened?

XX. If you know better than me . . .

AA. But of course I know better than you. Let's begin at the beginning. It is true that you went to the bus terminal. But not directly. This morning, when you got up and looked in the mirror to shave, as you do every Sunday, you didn't have the slightest intention of going there. When you had put on your suit and your pointed shoes . . . I've often asked myself why you wear those shoes, considering that they cripple your feet. Do you really think those pointed shoes conceal your peasant trotters? . . .

XX. (*piqued*) Those shoes cost a lot of money.

AA. Certainly. —Now, where did you go? Into the street. Everyone is free to go there. But those looks! . . . From a mile away people know who you are. Yes, you have the right to walk there, but they have the right to look at you. And to recognize your foreign mug. Because you're part of our people. Your flesh and blood belong to our people. And in this respect you are the pride of our idealists, even if very probably you don't know anything about it. You are something holy for our patriots, the sacred host of our national communion . . .

XX. Don't blaspheme!

AA. I'm speaking in metaphors.

XX. I don't give a damn, but I'm not going to let you insult religion.

AA. Let's go back to your walk. As you were passing the cinema you told yourself that you'd enjoy going in there.

XX. I love films.

AA. Of course. In the cinema nobody can look at you. Everybody is looking at the screen. You too. You watch something move, images, you don't understand anything that's being said. But that's of no importance. The essential thing is that you are there and that you feel safe. Unfortunately, the cinema has one flaw: you have to pay to get in.

XX. I never go to the cinema.

AA. That's right . . . But not all is lost. There are still parks, galleries, the railway station . . .

XX. And the bus terminal.

AA. Of course. The bus terminal. Given the choice, you take what is closest. So, you dash straight off to the

THE EMIGRANTS

terminal. And there everything is just right for you. First of all, the entrance is free. Secondly, there you are no longer a stranger. There are no strangers at a station, precisely because it has been made for strangers. At such a station your foreign ways are completely at home. In fact, at an international bus terminal, it's the locals who look like foreigners. And besides, a bus terminal is well lit, well heated . . . there are newsstands, public telephones, wickets . . .

XX. (*dreaming*) A restaurant . . .

AA. And a bar . . . as well. So you hung around the newsstand, the public telephones, the wickets . . .

XX. I had a beer.

AA. That I have my doubts about. A beer one has to pay for. On the other hand, I have no doubt that you went to the toilet . . .

XX. What about the platform?

AA. Let me finish! I'll get around to that.

XX. At first I went on the platform.

AA. Exactly. Physically, you first went on the platform and only afterwards to the toilet. But mentally, you elaborated the story of the platform after you'd been to the toilet, and there the urinal played an important, I'd even say a fertile role, it inspired you . . .

XX. Are you trying to say that I never went out on the platforms?

AA. But of course you did. And there were buses lined up on the platforms, one was just arriving, an international bus with a dog on the side, the passengers got off. All that is true. And it is equally true that a young woman, beautiful, elegant, got off last . . .

XX. See what I mean?

AA. Yes, all that you've seen alright. And afterwards you went to pee. Because it's free and because you can't get over the fact that here the toilets are cleaner than our baptismal fonts.

XX. Don't blaspheme!. The urinal was blocked.

AA. It's true, on holidays the service is rather lax.

XX. The bowl was full of cigarette butts.

AA. There you are! So you contemplated the butts bobbing in the torrent of urine. There you find men reaching into their trousers with religious awe, each rummaging in his own trousers, each by himself and yet joined together in a sort of communion of promiscuous evacuation. You inhale those reassuring fumes. They don't disgust you. On the contrary. Do you know any other place where your neighbour finds himself in exactly the same situation as you? Where else does such incomparable equality exist? Nowhere. Naturally, you are incapable of comprehending that this is an equality of debasement. Such nuances escape you. To you, what is coarse is authentic. — So, you stayed there a long time. . . . Unfortunately, you couldn't stay there forever. Once you had finished your business, when you had stopped pretending you were still at it, and after you had run your comb through your hair — by the way, it's remarkable to observe the extent to which, in your case, urology is connected with cosmetic care — so then you left your little cubicle, and it was at this point that the idea was born in your head — remarkable, too, the extent to which cosmetic care stimulates your brain functions: one wonders if the action of the teeth of the comb on your cranium has something to do with it — anyway, it was then that this naive and stupid little lie was born in your heart your amorous adventure with the woman who got off the bus last . . .

XX. I followed her . . .

AA. Nonsense. Oh, you stood by the bus alright and

burnt your fingers. But that cigarette butt is the closest you've ever come to freedom. Apart from that, you know only desire, hatred, envy, hero-worship, humiliation. . . . Of course you daydream of women, but they remain a terrible mystery to you because your sexuality has never developed beyond its primary functions. Which is why the toilet was precisely the place to stimulate your sexual fantasies to dream up an imaginary —

XX. Stop it!

AA. Why? Isn't that the way things happened?

XX. No!

AA. Don't worry. Next week you can go back to the bus terminal. (*XX takes an empty bottle of beer which was standing on the table, breaks it at the edge of the table and brandishes the jagged neck of it. Both AA and XX get up.*) Alright, alright! You had her, you made love to her. She gave herself to you, she threw herself at your feet, she kissed your hands, she kissed your feet, she embraced your pointed shoes, she groveled before you, she adored you, you and your pointed shoes. She . . . the ambassador, and even the ambassador's limousine with the little flag! The ambassador bowed to you and they're going to have fireworks in your honour . . . and afterwards they'll buy you an ice cream. Because you are beautiful! The whole world admires you. Are you content? Feeling better? Is that enough? (*XX sits down and puts the broken bottleneck on the table. Pause.*) You want some tea? (*conciliatory*) I can make you some tea.

XX. Do you have to spoil everything?

AA. Are you angry?

XX. What do you want with me?

AA. You are upset because what I said was true.

XX. You're always after me. I've never done you any harm . . .

AA. What do you want, my dear? I am merely helping you wake up to our situation, because on your own you're incapable . . .

XX. What situation? I went to the bus terminal.

AA. That demonstrates your situation.

XX. I wanted to feel good.

AA. That's it. It's always like that with us: We embellish the facts, we take our dreams for reality, we're full of pious hopes . . . A falsified present produces a sick future. History takes its revenge.

XX. What history?

AA. Ours, the history of our people.

XX. I went to the bus terminal.

AA. Right. And that's part of history. A small part, it's true. You *went* to the bus terminal—past tense, therefore history. History consists of such small individual incidents. There's no history in the abstract. Only idealists think so. They treat history as though it were a new god. But I'm not a Hegelian. Everything depends on how we interpret your little story. Are we going to examine it in the light of facts? Or are we going to examine the facts in the light of history?

(*Suddenly a loud gurgling sound issues from the pipes which pass through the room. AA makes a resigned gesture and sits down, thoughtfully, on his bed. XX stretches and yawns.*)

XX. I'm hungry.
AA. Eat, and leave me in peace.
XX. There's nothing to eat.
AA. What about the tinned stuff?

XX. There aren't any more cans.

AA. You've wolfed them all down?

XX. Haven't you got any?

AA. Yes, but I'm not giving you any more.

XX. Why not?

AA. For didactic reasons.

XX. Mmmm. (*pause*) What's that supposed to mean?

AA. It means that you're always wolfing down my tins of food.

XX. That's not true. Mine as well.

AA. Yours and mine. It's time you acquired a little order, discipline, loyalty . . .

XX. Okay, but first I want to have something to eat.

AA. Not from me.

XX. Nothing?

AA. Nothing.

XX. It doesn't matter. (*pause*) Weren't you talking about tea?

AA. You'll have to make it yourself. (*XX gets up, takes off his jacket, and hangs it over the back of his chair after having carefully dusted it. He disappears behind the screen. One hears him busying himself. He puts water on to boil. He returns and sits down. Pause.*)

XX. Tell me, why aren't there any flies here?

AA. (*jolted from his dreams*) What?

XX. I'm asking you why there aren't any flies.

AA. Where?

XX. Here, in this room.

AA. (*still a little distracted*) I don't know.

XX. There aren't any out in the hall either, none at all. (*pause*) Nowhere. (*over-excited by his discovery*) You tell me, have you seen any, around here, flies I mean?

AA. I don't think so. Not in winter anyway.

XX. Well, I'm telling you there aren't any. Neither in here, nor outside. There are no flies at all. Why aren't there any flies?

AA. I have no idea. Perhaps they've been exterminated. For hygienic reasons.

XX. Pity.

AA. But why do you need flies?

XX. It makes you feel better. You can catch them. You can watch them . . . It makes the time pass quicker. At home, we had flies. In the summer . . . (*pause*) There were always flies. And fly-paper. I remember, we used to hang it by the light. They looked as if they were covered with honey, but it wasn't honey. Anyway, they stuck to it and they buzzed. And when the fly-paper had been up a long time there were so many of them it was just one loud buzz, like music. Some had a deep buzz, some a high one, because for instance when you had a wasp or a hornet . . . No, the hornets worked themselves free, they were too strong . . . I remember . . . I remember —

AA. I remember, I remember, I remember! — I remember nothing!

XX. (*sincerely surprised*) What d'you mean? You don't remember?

AA. (*jumps up from his bed and begins to walk up and down*) No, I remember nothing, and I don't want to remember! It's always the same story: "You remember this? You remember that? . . ." Always, eternally, forever, after all these years! Now it's flies, you and your flies . . .

XX. Well . . . there were lots of them.

AA. Stop it!

XX. What d'you mean? You want me to say there weren't any when there were?

AA. There were flies, there were . . . So what? Does

THE EMIGRANTS

that mean that till the end of my days I have to remember a lot of stupid flies. I have other things to think about.

XX. You see. Now you admit there were flies.

AA. Oh shit! I never said there weren't any. Listen. The issue is not whether there were flies or not. There were, there were, and now they're gone. Period. That's all. Now, there are other things.

XX. What, for example?

AA. How do you mean "what"?

XX. Yes, what? Perhaps you can tell me what other things . . .

AA. Everything! . . . Ehm . . . The world, its problems.

XX. What?

AA. I'm talking about ideas, phenomena, events . . .

XX. (*scornful*) Eeeh . . .

AA. Social, economical, political processes, cultural currents, the prodigious bustle of a humanity at the crossroad, a civilization in the midst of a profound change. The universal problems . . .

XX. But there are no flies.

AA. Fortunately. In fact, that's an apt metaphor. The flies symbolize the pettiness of the problems to which we were condemned back home. All those local problems, those petty problems . . . The petty chauvinisms, the petty reforms — all little nothings by little people in a little country. Here, at last, one can unfold one's wings.

XX. Like a little fly . . . Bzzzz . . .

AA. Confront the big problems! It's only in meeting great challenges that greatness is born. There's no victory without risk . . . Yes. You have to think big. On a big scale. It's true, for me there are no flies anymore. Thank God!

XX. For me there are.

AA. Where? Here?

XX. (*triumphant*) No, back home, in the old country. Don't you remember?

AA. Oh no! Here you go again. (*A whistling sound is heard behind the screen.*)

XX. The water's boiling. (*He gets up and goes behind the screen. He returns carrying an aluminum water kettle. He pours the water into a plastic tumbler and then drops a teabag into it.*)

AA. You could make me one too.

XX. Are you contributing the sugar?

AA. But I have already bought the tea.

XX. Yes, but there's no sugar. (*AA fetches a leather suitcase from under his bed; he produces a small key from his pocket, opens the suitcase and brings out a package of sugar; he closes and locks the suitcase, then puts the key back into his pocket and the suitcase under his bed. He puts the sugar on the table. He sits down at the table. XX tips the kettle over AA's plastic tumbler.*) There's no water left.

AA. Boil some more. (*XX slouches over to the tap. He turns it on, without result.*)

XX. There isn't any more.

AA. Without me you can do nothing. (*He goes to the sink and turns the tap on fully.*) You're right. There isn't any more water.

XX. There isn't any because none comes out.

AA. None comes out because there isn't any, imbecile.

XX. It's not my fault, is it? (*AA returns to the table and stands there. XX puts sugar in his tea.*)

AA. Are you going to drink that tea? (*XX nods.*) All by yourself? (*XX nods more vigorously.*) That's what I call solidarity. I thought that when your friend has

THE EMIGRANTS

nothing to drink . . . (*XX takes more sugar.*) That's too much sugar.

XX. I love sugar. (*He takes a little tea on his spoon, tastes it, adds more sugar and stirs his tea. AA takes a coin from his pocket.*)

AA. We are going to toss for it.

XX. What?

AA. To see who is going to drink the tea?

XX. Why?

AA. Because there is only one cup of tea, and we are two.

XX. But it's my tea.

AA. But I bought it.

XX. And I made it.

AA. Alright. Let's say the two of us have equal rights to it. — Heads or tails?

XX. Heads. (*AA throws the coin high in the air.*)

AA. Tails!

(*The coin falls on the floor and rolls under the bed on the right. Both of them get on the floor to look under the bed. It doesn't matter where the coin falls. The actors look for it as if it had rolled under the bed.*)

XX. Have you got it?

AA. Not yet. (*puts his hand under the bed*)

XX. (*pushing him away*) Let me.

AA. Wait a minute! (*brings out from under the bed a can of food*) What's that?

XX. That? . . . A can of food.

AA. Is it yours? But you have just finished telling me that you have no more cans . . . (*XX doesn't react.*)

Alright. In that case, since it doesn't belong to anyone, I'm going to take it.

XX. No! (*snatches the tin out of AA's hand*)

AA. You should be ashamed of yourself. To lie like this. (*sits down on the chair to the right and reaches for the cup of tea*) Are you so afraid of having to share with me? Your avarice is stronger than your gluttony. As if I needed your canned food. (*XX hides the can under his bed.*) There's no need to hide it. Your secret is out. You can happily indulge your vice now. Go ahead! Satisfy your savage and bestial appetite. No, not bestial. Animals never eat any more than they need. Your appetite is monstrous, pathological.

XX. You want any of it?

AA. No, thank you. Your canapés don't appeal to me. (*He drinks a mouthful of tea and immediately spits it out.*) Urrk! . . . It's too sweet!

XX. Well, I guess I'll eat a little . . .

AA. Bravo! You've conquered your avarice. There's some good in my method. Although it's debatable whether, in view of your avarice, your gluttony can be considered a virtue or vice versa.

XX. I'm going to eat.

AA. Eat, eat! I hope you enjoy it.

XX. Where's the can opener? . . . (*He gets very excited looking for the can opener.*)

AA. Tell me, why do you eat so much?

XX. Have you seen the can opener?

AA. Let's try and examine the question. There can be no doubt that in your case epicurism has nothing to do with it. So, what is it?

XX. It's disappeared. (*He disappears behind the screen.*)

AA. It's probably a question, quite simply, of the act

THE EMIGRANTS

of absorbing. We must assume that the absorption of food has a symbolic character. In absorbing nourishment, in the form of food, you absorb the surrounding environment. You absorb the world. (*XX emerges from behind the screen. He has an axe in his hand. He sits on the left side of the table opposite AA and tries to open the can with the axe.*) Yes, that's an attractive hypothesis. An act of substitution—or else . . . a magic act—that is to say, an act which realizes, in an arbitrary fashion, elements which are in fact, scientifically speaking, not identical. It's not so much a matter of food taking the place of everything else but of becoming reality itself. It would be interesting to compare my observations with certain data of contemporary anthropology concerning primitive civilizations. I'm afraid that the results of such a comparative study would establish a painful parallel between ritual cannibalism and—

XX. (*having finally succeeded in hacking open the can of food with brute force*) There!

AA. What d'you—?

XX. Take it! Eat!

AA. Why?

XX. So that you stop talking.

AA. You haven't understood what I said. Besides, I warned you beforehand, I don't want any. I feed myself in a balanced, rational manner.

XX. If you don't want any, there's no need to jabber on. (*XX reaches for the can of food.*)

AA. (*taking the can*) Wait! What is this?

XX. Meat. First grade.

AA. Where did you buy this?

XX. In a store.

AA. What store?

XX. A regular store. —Give it back to me.

AA. (*putting on his glasses*) This is a can of dogfood.

XX. What d'you mean – dogfood? (*AA reads the label.*)

AA. "Non Plus Ultra". The All-Purpose Food for Domestic Animals. Healthy and Tasty . . . Prepared in our laboratories under the supervision of qualified veterinaries. A balanced diet consisting of all the necessary vitamins, proteins and minerals. Contains no harmful preservatives. A natural product, artificially coloured. Nutritious without producing side-effects like indigestion or obesity. Try it on your friend and watch the expression of love and loyalty grow in his eyes. *Nec Plus Ultra* – a Gift of Happiness for your four-legged friend!

XX. Well, all the same.

AA. "All the same" what?

XX. It says it's very good.

AA. Good – for dogs!

XX. It says nothing about dogs, it says 'friends' . . .

AA. "Your four-legged friends" – that means 'dogs'. It might include 'cats'.

XX. Impossible.

AA. Why "impossible"?

XX. Because it's meat. One doesn't give dogs meat.

AA. There's nothing contradictory in that. Dogs are animals, supreme carnivores.

XX. They've made a mistake somewhere.

AA. Of course not. Look, here, on top, it says clearly: "The All-Purpose Food for Domestic Animals" . . . And a little further down, look, they mention veterinaries . . . You are not convinced?

XX. Let me see. (*XX takes the can and scrutinizes it very closely. AA takes off his glasses and puts them back in the pocket of his dressing gown.*) No, I don't believe you.

THE EMIGRANTS

AA. Who speaks foreign languages here — you or me?

XX. You're saying all this only to annoy me.

AA. Alright. Look at the can. You see that picture? A dog, smiling, in front of a rising sun — the picture of happiness and satisfaction.

XX. So?

AA. What d'you mean "so"? The dog is smiling because he is going to eat a can of this product. Even an illiterate can understand a picture like that.

XX. A picture is only a picture. There are all kinds. Back home we had one in the parlour with a deer in a meadow and a sunset. The deer looks happy. So, is that supposed to mean it has come to devour the meadow?

AA. Perhaps.

XX. Never. A picture alone doesn't say anything. Pictures are for decoration. Yes. And this one tells you that the food in this can is very good. With such a nice picture —

AA. Naturally. — I presume you bought this can because of its price. You bought the cheapest can of food in the store.

XX. Finest quality.

AA. For dogs.

XX. Ultra-Super.

AA. Yes, of that I'm sure. We must keep our dogs happy.

XX. Well, anyway, I'm going to eat it!

AA. Am I stopping you?

XX. Just try.

AA. Why should I? It hasn't done you any harm so far. (*pause*) So, why don't you eat? (*XX, in a fit of temper, throws the can of food in a corner. He sulks. Pause.*)

XX. Because I'm not a dog.

AA. No?

XX. No!

AA. As you like. (*Pause. XX gets up and goes to pick up the can.*)

XX. Say . . . You tell me this is for cats too?

AA. Yes. "Domestic friends" — that includes cats.

XX. For sure?

AA. Definitely. But what difference does that make?

XX. Ah . . . Because if it's for cats, I can eat it. But if it's for dogs, no, out of the question! Do you think I'm a dog that I should eat dogfood?

AA. You are going to answer that right now.

XX. No, you tell me, you tell me yourself — am I a dog? Eh? Am I a dog?

AA. No. You're not. No man is a dog. Or at least, he shouldn't be.

XX. There you are! That means, if it's for cats I can eat it. Cats, that's a different matter. Cats are not dogs. Eh, tell me, can I eat it or not?

AA. You can . . . possibly . . .

XX. You sure I can?

AA. You can you can . . . (*Suddenly he starts to shout.*) Jesus fucking Christ! Eat what you want!! What difference does it make to me!

XX. That means I can? (*He starts to open the can with his axe.*)

AA. Leave it.

XX. But you've just told me I can eat it. (*AA pulls his suitcase out from under his bed. He unlocks it with the key and gets out a can of food. He slides the suitcase back under his bed, but without locking it. He puts the can of food on the table in front of XX.*) For people?

AA. For people.

XX. Well, that's different.

(*XX starts to open the can. There is the noise of people climbing stairs above their heads. Male voices, female laughter. AA puts his ear to one of the big pipes that passes vertically through their room.*)

AA. They're going up to the first floor. (*He moves away from the pipe.*) There's nothing like living in a basement. You hear absolutely everything through these pipes. The least noise, however quiet or intimate. Drainpipes, water pipes, the pipes for the central heating, the air conditioning, the sewage . . . I hear it all. I hear people come and go, prepare to go to bed and get up again. I hear them wash, flush the toilet. I hear them ventilate, relieve themselves, and propagate. However, up to now, I haven't heard anyone die yet. (*In the meantime XX has opened the can and has begun to eat.*)

XX. I guess they must be pretty healthy.

AA. Sometimes I have the impression we live in their stomach. Like microbes. No? Look at these pipes. Don't they remind you of bowels?

XX. They're pipes that look like pipes.

AA. Well, they remind me of intestines. We live like two bacteria in the interior of another organism. Two foreign bodies. Two parasites. Or worse still — what if we are two pathogenic microbes? The agents of decomposition in a healthy organism? Germs, Kock's bacilli, viruses, gonococci? I — a gonococcus! I, who have always considered myself a precious cell, a cell of highly developed cerebral matter, in fact, a particle that is no longer matter only, that is already superior to matter — and here I am: a gonococcus in the company of a protozoan!

XX. (*suspicious*) You talking about me?

AA. And on top of that, I can't stand basements! I hate them. Like all things subterranean. Everything that's underground gets on my nerves. It affects my psychology. I need sun, air, space. I'm a head person . . . And the head has to be held high in order to function normally. And as a superior link in the evolutionary process I wasn't made for caves. I've always lived on top floors and I've always had large vistas. From my windows. Here, there isn't even a single window.

XX. So much the better. You just get drafts from windows.

AA. Walls, nothing but walls and more walls!

XX. Yes, but at least they're warm. There are no drafts.

AA. The musty smell of basements.

XX. Nobody has ever died from that. But outside, in the fresh air, you can catch a cold. My father (God rest his soul), he lived in a basement, and he lived a long time.

AA. What did he die of?

XX. Pure air. One night he came home drunk and froze to death on the road.

AA. Well, can you survive down here?

XX. Why not? It's quite a decent apartment. It's warm here. And it's not expensive . . .

AA. That's true. And what's more it's me who pays the rent. Which reminds me, yesterday I paid another two months. November and December. And you owe me two months already. Altogether that makes four months.

XX. I haven't got a penny.

AA. You have only just been paid.

XX. But I don't have any money.

THE EMIGRANTS

(*On the floor above, the doorbell rings. The new arrivals are received with shouts of joy. The door is slammed.*)

AA. I don't understand what you do with your money. You must be earning at least as much as any average foreign labourer in this country. In fact, you earn one and a half times as much, seeing that you work twice as much. You're probably paid a special bonus as well, for the dangerous work you do. So, even if you are exploited and you're paid only half of all that, your earnings must still be well above the average income of a labourer. Yet, you live in the worst slum one can imagine, and since you live with me you pay only half the rent which is minimal to begin with. And you don't even pay that: when I ask you to pay what you owe me, you tell me you have no money.

XX. It's true. But you have some.

AA. I beg your pardon?

XX. You always have money.

AA. (*after a pause, icy:*) Do you realize what you are saying?

XX. Well what? Isn't it true?

AA. Do you realize that I might finally lose patience?

XX. Well, if you pay you've got to have money, no?

AA. Do you realize that I've already lost patience?

XX. Why? (*AA puts on his trousers, XX stops eating.*) You getting dressed? (*AA takes off his dressing gown and puts on his jacket.*) Where you going?

AA. I am moving out.

XX. (*relieved*) Hmmm . . . it's not the first time. (*Reassured, he goes back to his tin of food.*)

AA. (*tying his scarf in front of the mirror*) Up to now I have pitied you, but this time you've gone too far. You have just added chutzpah to plain dishonesty. I have had enough! I ask myself why I put up with you for such a long time. How could I have endured your boorish manners, your egotism, your filth. Even when you sleep you get on my nerves. Your snoring prevents me from sleeping and your carbonmonoxide gives me migraines. I pitied you, but now even pity won't stop me, because I have none left. Let me tell you, I've had enough of your company. Yes, enough! Up to here! I'm leaving!

XX. The key is under the mat.

AA. What did you say?

XX. I said the key'll be under the mat . . . In case you're coming back late . . .

AA. I'm not talking to you anymore. (*He puts on his coat, stops next to XX and turns to face him as he buttons his coat.*) You think I'm going to come back again? (*XX doesn't reply. He continues to chew his food calmly and pays not the slightest attention to AA. Getting no response, AA shrugs his shoulders and makes for the door. He puts his hand on the doorknob.*)

XX. Your shoes.

AA. What?

XX. You've forgotten to put on your shoes. You're not going to go out in the street in slippers, are you?

AA. I don't need your advice. (*AA returns to the middle of the room, puts on his shoes, goes back to the door and puts his hand on the knob. Pause.*) What makes you think I'd come back, if you don't mind my asking?

XX. Your bags.

AA. I beg your pardon.

XX. You've left your bags.

AA. So?

XX. It's obvious. If you were really moving out, you'd take your luggage.

AA. I admire your intelligence. But you're mistaken. I'm taking nothing with me.

XX. Exactly. That means you're not moving out.

AA. Oh yes? Well, I'm moving out. But I am taking nothing. I am leaving, that's true. But without taking anything. I am leaving everything behind although I am moving out. And despite the fact that I am going, I am taking nothing. I am simply leaving. I am moving out without taking anything. Now, is that clear?

XX. And your towels, your bedding, your clothes?

AA. You know very well that material objects, clothes and things are nothing in my eyes. I can do without them. I belong to the post-consumer society — unlike you.

XX. You're leaving everything? You're leaving everything for me?

AA. Ehm . . . perhaps not everything, come to think of it, maybe I'll take a little something as a souvenir . . . No, not everything. I'm going to take one thing, just a little thing that isn't worth much. (*He seems to be thinking.*) Now what could I . . . Let me see . . . That's it, I know! (*AA goes over to the bed on the right and takes the mascot, the dog PLUTO, a stuffed animal.*)

XX. No! (*XX rushes at AA.*)

AA. But why not? This innocent mascot will remind me of the times we spent together. It'll ease my nostalgia . . .

XX. You leave that alone.

AA. You're not fair. I'm leaving you everything I possess, in exchange I'm asking nothing but this little knick-knack as a souvenir; and you . . .

XX. Give it back to me!

AA. Let's go away from here, my pretty doggie. This gentleman is mean. This gentleman is nasty. This gentleman doesn't love us . . .

XX. Are you going to give it back to me or not?

AA. Come, my pet, let's leave this gentleman here. We'll go far away from here, far away . . . (*XX tries to snatch the stuffed dog, but AA succeeds in evading him and escaping to the other side of the table. They chase each other around the table.*) Wow! Wow! Look! . . . See how furious the gentleman is! Wow! Wow! Waw! Waw! (*He barks like a dog. The chase continues.*) Don't let him catch you! Run away! (*The moment XX is on the left of the table and AA on the right, XX jumps on the table and grabs AA by the throat. But only the scarf remains in his hands. AA jumps aside but trips over the chair and falls to the ground with the chair. XX throws himself on top of him. AA holds PLUTO up in the air with one hand. XX tries to catch it. AA changes the dog-mascot over into the other hand and throws it far behind himself. The two get up and rush after the mascot like two rugby players after the ball. They throw themselves violently on top of the dog. At this moment, the water starts to run from the tap which had remained turned on.*) Ah! The water! (*AA leaves his partner who clasps the dog-mascot covetously to his chest; AA goes over to the tap and turns it off.*) At last! Now I can make myself a decent cup of tea. (*AA takes the kettle from the table, fills it from the tap and disappears behind the screen. XX hasn't taken his eyes off him while clutching PLUTO very tightly to his chest in an apprehensive attitude. AA emerges from behind the screen.*) What are you doing down there? . . . You praying or something? (*He takes off his coat and hangs it up.*) Come on, that's enough . . . It's time you got up . . .

XX. You staying?

AA. Only because of the tea. Where else can you

THE EMIGRANTS

make a decent cup of tea if not at home. Ah, home, sweet home! (*XX gets up and hides the stuffed dog under his pillow, i.e. on the bed to the right. He sits down on his bed. AA picks up his scarf and puts it over the back of the left chair; then he picks up the overturned chair on the right.*)

XX. I'm going to pay you back as soon as I've got the money.

AA. Ah, you want to discuss the rent?

XX. Word of honour!

AA. It's a small matter. Not really worth talking about.

XX. Next month.

AA. There's no rush.

XX. Well, next week then.

AA. But no, please, don't think about it.

XX. Okay, the day after tomorrow.

AA. Oh!

XX. Is that alright, the day after tomorrow? . . . Or even tomorrow. You want it tomorrow?

AA. No, really, I assure you. It's of absolutely no importance. Between friends . . .

XX. Right now I can't. Word of honour . . .

AA. Aaah! How pleasant it is to be surrounded by all this furniture again . . . (*He prepares to take off his jacket. XX rushes to help him take it off.*)

XX. Shall I hang it up?

AA. Don't bother. It isn't worth it. Just put it over the chair. (*He seats himself comfortably in the chair on the left. XX hangs his jacket neatly over the back of the chair.*) In return, if you wouldn't mind . . . That light tires my eyes. It's been troubling me for a long time, but I didn't want to say anything since it didn't seem to bother you. Quite frankly, that naked bulb is atrocious.

Forgive me if I appear to be criticizing your interior decorating, but couldn't you make some sort of shade? From paper or something . . . I'm afraid I've never been particularly good with my hands.

XX. I'll make one for you.

AA. Perfect. You're really quite unique. Look, there are some magazines by my bed, use any of them. Unless you prefer ordinary newspaper.(*XX picks up a magazine from the floor by the bed on the left.*)

XX. I need scissors.

AA. They're on the shelf. (*XX fetches the scissors from the shelf above the sink. Then he climbs on the table, unfolds the magazine and tries to fasten it around the bulb. AA watches him, shading his eyes with one hand.*) This doesn't bother you?

XX. What?

AA. Can you look at the bulb without the disconcerting feeling that you're going blind?

XX. The bulb?

AA. The light. Doesn't it blind you?

XX. No.

AA. Doesn't it hurt your eyes?

XX. No.

AA. It doesn't make you cry?

XX. No.

AA. Your eyelids don't burn? And you don't see little black spots dancing before your eyes? (*a pause*)

XX. No. (*AA climbs on the table. He raises XX's eyelids with his fingers, like a doctor examining a patient's eyes.*)

AA. The other one. (*He looks into the other eye.*) Incredible! (*AA comes down from the table. XX continues to busy himself with the shade and the bulb. AA paces back and forth.*) Perhaps it's not so incredible

THE EMIGRANTS

after all. We know there can be considerable deviations from the norm. Both among those with hypersensitivity and those suffering from almost total apathy. It's the same with the speed of reflexes. From the ends of the nerve fibres to the centre of the brain. Everything depends on the individual. (*Suddenly he stops.*) Have you ever been interrogated?

XX. What?

AA. (*dry, brutal*) By the police?

XX. I haven't done anything.

AA. I'm not asking you if you've done anything. I'm asking you if you've ever been interrogated.

XX. No.

AA. (*resumes a normal tone*) What a pity! You would've made a perfect subject. Not from the point of view of the police, of course. Your insensitivity would've enabled you to endure things that would've broken others. It's a pity, a real pity. You would've made an excellent political prisoner.

XX. For me, politics —

AA. I know, I know, you keep out of politics. That's what you were going to say, right? One can always dream. (*XX is evidently interested in an ad in the magazine he is using for a shade. He licks his finger, turns the page and looks. . . .*) What eyes! It wouldn't be easy to extort a confession from you. That is, if you had anything to say . . . Too bad. The talent is wasted on you. It's always like that. Those who shouldn't say anything, talk. And those who would be able to keep their mouth shut, have nothing to say.

XX. Can I cut this out?

AA. What?

XX. This section here, with all the colours.

AA. You haven't listened to a word I was saying.

XX. (*showing him an ad in full colour*) If I could cut out this ad — just this one . . .

AA. Oh, my god! I keep asking myself if the god of my forefathers was the same as the one yours worshipped.

XX. I'm going to cut it out then.

(*XX climbs down from the table and sits on the chair to the right, facing the audience. He cuts out the ad. From above we hear music.*)

AA. (*puts his head between his hands and covers his ears*) That's all we need! (*He looks at his watch.*) Four o'clock? That's impossible. (*He puts his watch to his ear.*) Just as I thought. It's stopped. Say, what time d'you think it might be?

XX. Around nine o'clock.

AA. That means they've only just started. They're going to celebrate for at least 8 hours . . . It's *their* party!

XX. Perhaps they're going to stop early.

AA. No, not tonight. They're not going to stop. They're going to have fun till dawn. It's New Year's Eve. (*The water kettle whistles behind the screen.* Ah, the water! (*AA disappears behind the screen and returns with the kettle. He sits on his chair, pours the water into his plastic tumbler and drops the teabag into it. XX drops his arms, the scissors in one hand, the magazine in the other. Above them, the music fades. AA fishes the teabag out of his tumbler, puts sugar in his tea and stirs. XX lets the scissors and the magazine drop to the floor. He gets up slowly and walks like an automaton over to his bed (on the right). There he drops down on his back and stares at the ceiling. AA stops stirring his tea and looks attentively at XX.*) What's the matter with you? . . . Don't you feel well? (*He stirs his tea, then stops again.*) Are you ill? (*XX doesn't react. AA gets up and approaches him.*) Hey — why don't you answer? (*He shakes XX by the arm whereupon he rolls over to face the wall, turning his back to AA. AA appears to give up. He picks up the scissors and the magazine and goes back to XX.*) Hey, you haven't finished. . . . Here! It's all yours. Take it, cut, cut as much as you want — the fridges, the vacuum cleaners, the cars and motorcycles, the transistor radios and outboard motors, the telephones and intercoms, the TVs and VDs — it's stupid, but I'm not stopping you. Go ahead, cut all you like! . . . It goes without saying that you may do as you please . . . You have my permission . . . D'you hear? What's the matter? Are you annoyed or something? (*He sits down on the bed.*) If you want me to, I'll cut them out for you . . . Say something! D'you want me to cut them out for you? (*He cuts the colour ads out of the magazine and then puts the scissors on the floor.*) Well, there it is . . . It's done. They're nice, don't you think? (*He holds the ads at arm's length and looks at them with a grin.*) Hey, look at them! . . . (*enraged*) You might at least look! Who d'you think I've cut them all out for? . . . Why don't you answer? . . . Are you manic-depressive? (*For a moment he sits without moving. Through the pipes we hear "Stille Nacht, Heilige Nacht", or "Minuit Chrétien", sung by a children's choir. Abruptly, XX buries his head in his pillow.*) Aha . . . so that's it! (*AA gets up and looks around. He is evidently considering something. Then he makes a decision. He takes everything that's on the table and puts it on the floor close to the wall. He empties the tea into the sink and rinses the tumblers. He goes to his bed, takes the pillowcase off his pillow and spreads it across the table like a table cloth. Then he fetches a bottle of cognac from his suitcase and puts it on the table. He places a package of cigarettes, which he had hidden under his pillow, next to the bottle. He puts the tumblers alongside. Then he dons his jacket. During that time the music has slowly faded.*) It's ready! . . . Hey! Wake up! . . . It's ready!

XX. (*sticking his head out from under his pillow*) What is it?

AA. (*solemnly*) The New Year. (*XX covers his head again with his pillow. AA pulls it away.*)

XX. Leave me in peace!

AA. Out of the question! I'm not going to drink by myself.

XX. (*defending himself*) I don't want any tea.

AA. Who is talking of tea? I have something better, for such an occasion.

XX. (*Seeing the bottle, he sits up.*) Where did you get that?

AA. Never mind! I am treating you . . . Put on your jacket!

XX. What for?

AA. Because this is a festive occasion . . . A feast, a ball, a ceremony, a celebration, a cult, a custom, a ritual! Our goodbye to the year that's passing away . . . We welcome the New Year, a new era, a new life, everything is new. Alleluia! You are not going to stay in your shirt sleeves for such an elegant party, are you? . . . Come on! Get up, move, enjoy yourself! . . . (*He forces XX to get up and leads him to the table. He takes the jacket which hangs over the chair on the right and gives it to XX.*) Straighten your tie! Button up! Comb yourself! After all, you don't want the New Year to be sick at the sight of you, do you?

THE EMIGRANTS

XX. You don't have a tie.

AA. Me? . . . Yes, that's true.

XX. So then?

AA. Yes, but it's different in my case. I never wear a tie. It's not my style. (*XX takes off his jacket, hands it to AA and goes back to his bed.*) Wait. (*XX lies down on his bed again.*) Is it really necessary? Really? Do I have to?

XX. If it's a party, it's a party . . .

AA. Very well. (*AA goes to his bed; on the way he hangs the jacket of XX over the chair on the right. He fetches his suitcase from under his bed, opens it, and brings out a tie. He puts on the tie in front of the mirror. XX watches him, then gets up and goes to sit on the chair to the right. He pulls a handkerchief from his pocket and uses it to polish his shoes. AA turns to him with his tie.*) Is that alright now?

XX. (*after taking a long look*) When is the last time you shaved?

AA. I don't remember.

XX. Yes, exactly. You need a shave.

AA. Ah, no! You're not going to ask me to shave right now.

XX. If I can do it, you can do it too, no?

AA. Nowadays it isn't necessary to shave anymore.

XX. Not every day, no. But a holiday is different . . .

AA. Okay, I'm prepared to shave. But on one condition.

XX. What?

AA. That you change your socks.

XX. (*Who looks, with astonishment, at his feet; he is wearing socks full of holes.*) Why? They're still quite clean . . .

AA. It's either that or nothing.

XX. If I put on my shoes, you can't see anything.

AA. It's an ultimatum.

XX. Okay, okay . . . (*XX gets a suitcase made of pressed paper out from under his bed and brings out a pair of socks. He takes off his old socks and puts them in the suitcase. He puts on the new pair of socks — they have at least as many holes as the old ones. During that time AA takes off his jacket and hangs it over the chair on the left. He stops in front of the mirror and starts to shave. Waiting for AA to finish his shave, XX remains seated, without moving. He continues to watch AA. He smiles.*) I can't wait till it's spring.

AA. Why?

XX. Because, I tell you, in spring some women go without panties.

AA. Here we go again.

XX. It's true, I'm telling you . . . We're digging ditches now, laying sewage pipes.

AA. I don't see the connection.

XX. Come on. When one of them walks by up above, you can get a look from below.

AA. So that's how the common man gets his kicks.

XX. Just now we're working in a posh district. Working in the eastend isn't worth the effort. You see few people, and the women are either ugly or old. But where we are now we get the elegant ones . . . in fur coats and such. One of us is always on the look-out. He gives us a signal when a juicy one is coming. The best place is outside a department store, near the lingerie section. Or by a ladies hairdresser. One time, I remember, we were laying cables in front of a chic restaurant . . . the ideal depth — one and a half meters. Up above there was only a small plank . . . Oh, my God! I thought I'd twist my neck. That was a fine place to work . . . You should come some day.

AA. No, thank you. I have other possibilities.

XX. The worst was when we worked outside an army barracks. For two whole weeks we saw nothing but uniforms.

AA. Does your wife go to the hairdresser?

XX. No, of course not.

AA. To the restaurant?

XX. What d'you think? Where I come from you eat at home.

AA. She goes shopping then.

XX. Yes. (*a pause*) But back home, in our village, there are no sewage pipes or water mains.

AA. But there's an army barrack.

XX. Yes. How d'you know?

AA. It's easy. Back home there are army barracks everywhere. – So, perhaps she walks past the barracks.

XX. Yes?

AA. Your wife. (*a pause*)

XX. What's that supposed to mean?

AA. Nothing. I've finished. (*rinses his face and then dries himself with his towel*) Now, let's celebrate! (*XX gets up. Facing each other, they put on their jackets simultaneously, AA to the left and XX to the right of the table. Then they sit down at the same time. AA opens the bottle and fills their glasses.*)

XX. Were you married?

AA. Twice.

XX. How so?

AA. I was divorced . . . Cheers!

XX. Children?

AA. What children? – Oh, no, I have no children.

XX. So, why did you get married?

AA. What d'you mean – 'why'? For love . . . Because our minds met – is that good enough? Come on, drink! (*They drink. AA takes a cigarette and offers XX the package. XX takes a cigarette too. AA searches his pockets for matches. XX gets a box of matches out of his right pocket, but puts it back right away. He gets another box out of his left pocket, gives AA a light and then lights his own cigarette. He puts the box of matches back into his left pocket. The two of them inhale. Pause.*)

XX. Tell me, why did you run away?

AA. (*his thoughts interrupted*) What?

XX. Why did you run away from the Old Country? Weren't you well off there? You had two women, a home in the big city . . . You made a good living, you moved in the best circles, lots of VIP's I bet . . . And here?

AA. One doesn't run away towards something . . . One runs away from something.

XX. Exactly. But back home you were better off than here.

AA. One day I was walking in the park. There were children having fun on the playground. Suddenly I saw a boy a little older than they, hiding behind a lilac bush. He was picking up stones and throwing them at the children and then quickly hiding again behind the lilac bush. He gave me the impression of someone sneering at the world. He was perfectly content doing that, even cheerful. A strapping boy, strong clever . . . Each time he threw a stone he hid behind the lilac bush. (*a pause*)

XX. How old was he?

AA. Probably around ten or twelve.

XX. (*moved*) Same age as mine.

AA. Yes. It could've been your son. (*a pause*)

XX. And after that?

AA. Nothing. That's all.

XX. Sure, sure . . . And now tell me the truth.

AA. That is the truth.

THE EMIGRANTS

XX. You're not going to tell me that you emigrated because some brat threw stones in a park. He didn't even throw them at you. So, out with it. You can talk to me like a brother.

AA. Well, let's say . . . let's say I always had a problem with diction. For instance, the word "generalissimo" . . . It's too difficult for me. I've never succeeded in pronouncing it correctly.

XX. You? But you've got an education.

AA. Well, yes. Maybe it's not so much a question of diction as of intonation, of the right note . . . I always sang out of tune.

XX. (*in a low voice, confidentially*) Are you . . . a political refugee?

AA. You could call it that. (*XX gets up from the table.*) You mean you never had any idea? (*XX goes towards the door and stops, turning his back on AA.*)

XX. And you tell me that only now?

AA. I thought it was clear from the beginning. (*XX half opens the door with infinite care, furtively sticks his head out, closes the door and comes back to the table.*)

XX. Are you on the list?

AA. Probably. (*XX remains standing, undecided.*) What are you standing for?

XX. (*sitting down*) I was a fool! (*hits his forehead with his fist*) Still, from the beginning I thought there was something suspicious about you. He does nothing; he doesn't go to work; he lies on his bed all day long, reading. And those soft hands, well groomed . . . An intellectual!

AA. How do you know I don't do anything? Because you think that work consists only of digging ditches with a pneumatic drill?

XX. Okay, you tell me what you do on that bed?

AA. I think.

XX. (*irritated and scornful*) Yeah . . . What about?

AA. You, for instance. I ask myself if you would be capable of being an informer.

XX. A what?

AA. That is to say, could you denounce me? Not now, of course, and not here. But back home in the Old Country . . .

XX. Back home we wouldn't have known each other.

AA. You think one can only denounce people one knows, or friends? No. Listen. Let's assume you are in prison and I come to suggest you escape. Or better still, I come to you with a plan to free all the prisoners. What would you do? Would you call the guards and hand me over to them?

XX. In what prison?

AA. In a prison where you're not that badly off. Maybe better than outside, free. Where you have enough to eat, where you're never cold.

XX. I've never heard of a prison like that.

AA. But a prison where one thing is forbidden, one single thing. It is forbidden to use words that start with the letter P. All words that start with a P are forbidden. Both in spoken and in written language.

XX. Why?

AA. So that nobody can write or speak the word 'prison'. You can have recourse to allusions or to synonyms. But the word 'prison' is forbidden. It's forbidden to say it, to write it, even to think it.

XX. That's not a prison.

AA. Well, if I were to propose to you . . .

XX. (*jumps up*) What in hell d'you want from me?

AA. I don't want anything! I merely ask myself what would have happened if I had actually proposed to . . .

THE EMIGRANTS 43

XX. I have a wife and children!

AA. And I, I've . . . I've . . . Come to think of it, what do I have? Let's say I have my words . . . my dear, my beloved words, words that begin with all the letters of the alphabet. No, I am not proposing anything, I am not suggesting anything to you . . . Come on, sit down, and let's drink! You are not in any danger with me. I am a political refugee alright, but I am not an agitator. (*XX sits down. AA pours drinks.*) Here you are! A toast to common sense and simple minds! Prosit! Skol! Cheers! Down the hatch! Tchin tchin! (*XX doesn't drink.*) Don't be afraid! I'm just a dishrag. A coward. And perhaps, from a normal, simple human point of view – a bastard. . . . Come on, drink! . . . We're by ourselves. (*XX puts his glass down.*) Why aren't you drinking? (*XX is silent.*) I understand. Now you think I'm a government agent.

XX. Eh, no!

AA. Admit it. I said I was a bastard, so you conclude I must be a government agent, right? (*XX is silent. AA raises his glass.*) Shall we drink? (*XX doesn't react.*) Well, well. You know, if you take a dislike to a loyal servant of your government, that raises certain doubts in your loyalty to the regime. That's bad, that's very bad, my friend. What if I really were a government spy?

XX. I never said that.

AA. But you thought it. So why not say it out loud? What harm would it do? (*XX remains silent. A pause.*) Hmm. I'm beginning to understand. You've decided that if my mission is secret, you as a loyal citizen must not let on that you have any knowledge of it. Very good. A loyal subject should always pretend to suspect nothing. Bravo! Now you should also make my task a little easier by attacking the government a little. A few seditious ideas? A little criticism of the regime? How about it?

... Don't feel constrained on my account. In the presence of a government agitator, a loyal citizen must not be too loyal, precisely to prove his loyalty.

XX. I don't understand what you're talking about.

AA. That's not important. I appeal to your common sense. Drink with me! — to prove that you're on the side of the regime! Remember I can report you to the authorities if I'm a secret government agent.

XX. I don't want to drink with you.

AA. Careful! I represent the State . . . the government . . . the regime . . . political power —

XX. It's not because of that.

AA. But why then?

XX. Because you said you were a bastard.

AA. Exactly. So what?

XX. Well, that's all, it's because of that.

AA. You mean you don't want to drink with a bastard?

XX. Oh, why shouldn't I? Of course I can drink with a bastard. That's not the point. It's because you said that here we're among ourselves. That means that I too am a bastard.

AA. So, then, you don't consider yourself a bastard?

XX. No.

AA. Which means you think you're better than I.

XX. That's not true. It's just that I don't see why I should be a bastard. What have I done for you to treat me like that? Tell me, why do you treat me like a bastard? (*AA is silent.*) If you don't know why, you should shut up instead of insulting me. One doesn't go around insulting people without reason. (*a pause*)

AA. Alright. Let's say I exaggerated a little.

XX. In that case, it's different. That means we're not among ourselves here.

AA. Let's say — not quite.

XX. (*delighted*) But that changes everything. I can drink with you now.

AA. That suits me fine.

XX. (*relieved*) So, let's drink.

AA. We've settled our differences.

XX. Right. (*They clink glasses and drink.*)

AA. You know, it's strange . . . I wonder why I'm the only one of us who could possibly be a government agent?

XX. Oh, stop it!

AA. Which means that only I could ever be suspected. The idea of suspecting you of being a government agent would never enter my head.

XX. Will you stop it, please!

AA. Alright. I shan't insist.

XX. How long is it till midnight?

AA. I don't know. My watch has stopped.

XX. Maybe we could ask somebody.

AA. No. It's not worth the trouble. They're going to drink champagne upstairs. We shall hear the corks pop at midnight.

XX. Yeah . . . And at home, they're waiting for me. Like every year. The children are waiting for me, they're hoping I'll come back . . . And once again I won't be there. Ah, what a life . . . what a life!

AA. But why haven't you gone back for a visit? You can . . . You're not a political refugee. You could go home for your holidays.

XX. Holidays? Me? I never get a holiday.

AA. But you could ask for one.

XX. Good God! You think I'm here to have holidays? I'm here to make money. I shall take a holiday when I get back. A whole week. I shall wrap myself in a blanket, lie down in the orchard, and I shall sleep. I won't as much as move a little finger. Now and again I'll open one eye to make sure the sky is still there and then I go back to sleep. There'll only be the wife to bring me food. And after . . .

AA. Well, after that?

XX. After, I'll get up and get dressed. In style. Nothing but clothes from abroad.

AA. Why?

XX. What d'you mean "why"? Because it'll be my birthday.

AA. Your birthday?

XX. Sure. My birthday happens to be in May. I'll invite the whole village. Oh, I don't mean everybody. There are some I don't like; they don't get invited. That'll teach them. — We'll kill a pig, a calf, or maybe a cow . . . And I'm going to buy plenty of liquor . . . enough for everybody, and even to have some left over — I want them to have a good time, enjoy themselves, so they know I've come back from abroad. We'll spread everything out in the hall. For everybody to see. But not to touch, mind you. Just to look at. I'm going to ask my brother-in-law to watch things. Not that you can trust him either.

AA. You could get a dog.

XX. A dog?

AA. Yes, a watch-dog. He wouldn't let anyone touch a thing. You'd tie him up, of course, so that he couldn't steal what he was supposed to guard.

XX. That's a good idea. — After that, we'll have a party that lasts three days.

AA. That I don't doubt.

XX. And when the party is over, you know what I'm going to do then?

AA. Obviously, you're going to clean up after the guests.

XX. Like hell I will. My mother-in-law'll do that. No. I'm going to build my house.

AA. No?!

XX. Yes. A beautiful house. In stone. Two storeys. And with central heating.

AA. You must be joking.

XX. The most beautiful house in the village. With my own money.

AA. That's going to take a while.

XX. Several years. But when I'm finished, we're going to move out of our in-laws' place and go to live by ourselves. In our own house. Eh? So what d'you think of that?

AA. It's a fine project . . . (*He gets up and raises his glass.*) Well . . . To your house!

XX. To my house! (*They drink. Suddenly, the hand in which XX holds his glass begins to tremble.*)

AA. Watch out! You're going to upset your glass. Hold on, goddammit, you're going to spill half of it! What's the matter with you? (*XX is unable to hold his glass and puts it on the table. He sits facing the audience, turning his profile to AA who puts his glass on the table too and goes over to XX.*) Let me see your hands. (*XX puts his hands in his pockets.*) Let me see your hands! (*Reluctantly, XX takes his hands out of his pockets.*) Show me! (*XX stretches out his arms, clenching his fists.*) Not like this! Straighten them! (*AA forcibly opens his fists. XX turns away his head as he holds out his arms in front of AA. His hands shake in jerks. AA turns aside without looking at him. XX puts his hands back into his pockets.*) Have you had this for long?

XX. A year.

AA. Often?

XX. No. Just every once in a while.

AA. More and more frequently? (*XX is silent.*) I am asking you if this happens more and more frequently. (*XX is silent. AA takes his glass, goes to stand behind him and with his left arm gives him a twist that forces him to tilt his head backward. He pushes the glass against his mouth. XX drinks the content of the glass. AA replaces the empty glass on the table and picks up his own full glass. He empties it in one gulp and then puts it back on the table.*)

XX. (*coughing and spitting*) Thanks very much.

AA. Why don't you learn the language? (*XX goes on coughing, though now deliberately, in order to gain time.*) I am asking you why you don't learn the language?

XX. What language?

AA. The language people here speak.

XX. (*Takes his hands out of his pockets and looks at them: they are still trembling.*) It's going to go away soon. (*puts his hands back in his pockets*)

AA. Are you going to answer me or what?

XX. You mean why don't I speak their language?

AA. You know damn well what I mean. You're an illiterate in this country — worse, a deafmute!

XX. I don't want to learn their language.

AA. Why not? You live in this country. You eat here, you drink, you walk the streets like people here — so why don't you want to speak like them? You could get a better job . . .

XX. They're not people.

AA. No?

XX. No. They're not human. There aren't any real people here.

AA. And where, according to you, are these real people?

XX. Back home.

AA. Ah, yes . . .

XX. (*takes his hands out of his pocket and looks at them*) It's over. (*puts his hands back into his pockets*)

AA. Do you know what happens to people who work with a pneumatic drill for too long?

XX. They age more quickly.

AA. Not only.

XX. They go a little deaf. (*He takes one hand out of his pocket and puts a finger in his ear.*) After a while I get a buzz in my ear. I don't hear very well anymore.

AA. That's normal. But there are other things.

XX. (*takes his finger out of his ear and his other hand out of his pocket*) It's over now. (*puts his hands back into his pockets*)

AA. The buzzing?

XX. No . . . My hands.

AA. That's nothing. And the noise in your ear is nothing either. There's worse to come. As a result of exposure to the vibrations for ten hours a day, certain modifications occur in the conjunctive tissue, that is to say, in the tissue by which the flesh is attached to the bone. How long have you had this?

XX. (*looks at his outstretched arms*) They've stopped shaking.

AA. I'm asking you how long you've been working with this machine.

XX. Three years.

AA. These modifications of the conjunctive tissue constitute a process of degeneration. In other words, the flesh begins to detach itself from the bones . . . The consequence is, of course, a total incapacity to work.

XX. Are you serious?

AA. Sickness and disability. It's a question of

medically established facts. It's a terrible occupational disease.

XX. (*He's afraid.*) Eh, don't give me all this bullshit. You're just trying to scare me.

AA. (*seizing XX by his lapels*) You think you're a man, don't you? Well, you're nothing but an animal. You're not a human being at all. Not even a bastard! You're neither man nor dog, that's for sure! . . . A calf. Worse, an ox! A dull, helpless, stupid ox! A complete ox. Good only for pulling a plough till the moment you drop dead . . . Pulling a plough — that's what makes you happy! And you can't get enough of it! . . . You're happy, right? You're happy, no? (*He shakes XX.*)

XX. Don't shake me!

AA. (*shakes him*) I'll shake you till you wake up from your bovine dream. Because when you don't work you sleep . . . or you chew the cud. I shall go on shaking you and shouting at you till I've made a man of you. And I shan't stop till I've achieved that. Because as long as you remain an ox I'll be a bastard. The one goes with the other. The ox and the bastard. And I'll be the vilest of bastards so long as you're an ox in his yoke. There's no other way.

XX. (*menacing*) Don't shake me! I'm warning you! . . .

AA. You are going to defend yourself? It doesn't make any difference. Some day you're going to understand . . . and then you'll be grateful to me. Because it's not possible for only one of us to be a man. It's either both of us or neither. (*He launches into a lyrical flight of speech, partly under the influence of the alcohol he's drunk. He continues to hold XX by the lapels.*) And when at last both of us can stand on our own two feet, we shall stand upright. We shall raise our heads. And then we shall see above us a branch, gently swaying. A branch bearing fruit. The forbidden fruit! And the wind that moves that branch is the wind of history. And we hold out our hand and . . . (*XX slaps his hands. AA drops his jacket and staggers back.*)

XX. Don't you touch me! (*He gets up.*) Who are you raising your hand against? Who? Eh?

AA. Don't you understand?

XX. What? You raised your hand against me! Against me! (*Furious, he goes towards AA.*) You goddam louse, you arsehole, you son of a bitch! . . . You're going to see . . .

(*He raises his arm, ready to strike AA. The light goes out. Total darkness. Up above we hear people exclaim in chorus: the typical "Aaah" of surprise people produce when it suddenly turns dark. Then the sound of a trumpet and of whistling. At the same time a clock strikes twelve. In the distance bells begin to toll.*)

AA. (*voice only: in the dark*) Midnight!

XX. (*voice only*) Why has the light gone out?

AA. They turn them off at midnight on New Year's Eve. That's the custom here. (*a pause*) You have any matches? (*XX strikes a match. AA goes behind the screen and returns with a candlestick. He lights the candle with the match which XX holds. He puts the candle on the table and turns to XX.*) Good.

XX. (*scratches his neck with an embarrassed air*) Ehm well . . .

AA. Now then, we could . . .

XX. As you like . . .

AA. In that case . . .

XX. Yes . . . ehm . . .

AA. Of course . . .

XX. Why not . . .

AA. Certainly . . .

XX. Sure . . .

AA. Well, let's drink . . . (*He pours new drinks.*) To the New Year!

XX. (*raising his glass*) To the New Year! (*They clink glasses and empty them. They are still a little stiff, embarrassed, uneasy. They sit down, AA on the chair to the left, XX on the right.*) Listen to the bells!

AA. Church bells.

XX. Well, I wish you . . .

AA. Likewise . . .

XX. The past . . . is the past.

AA. Let's forget all that . . . (*offers XX his hand*)

XX. Well then. . . . I guess we should . . . (*extends his hand to AA*)

AA. All the best . . .

XX. Happy New Year! (*They shake hands across the table. They light their cigarettes, as before, following the same scenario, with one difference: XX does not go through his number with the two boxes of matches. They make themselves comfortable. From that moment on they are visibly under the influence of alcohol, especially XX.*) Eeeh . . . new year — how time passes! . . . Everything passes . . . I remember . . . it's a long time ago, I was still a boy, I tended the cows. I used to climb trees to take the eggs out of the crows' nests . . . I went to school barefoot. But only in the fall. In the spring there was too much work in the fields. And in the winter it was too cold. Then my father left for the city. But my grandparents stayed. Old people are funny. They prefer to stay. It was a wretched life, but they stayed. I guess they must've loved all that misery, eh?

AA. That's not for me to judge.

THE EMIGRANTS

XX. Well, I didn't love it. (*strikes his forehead*) And no one's ever going to make me say that I loved it.

AA. Who, in his right mind, loves misery?

XX. My father didn't either. He loved it so little that he drank away all the money he earned. And after that he loved it even less. So he went on drinking . . . But me, I don't drink.

AA. That's good.

XX. Because I hate poverty. I like having things. When I hold something in my hands then I have it. And when I let it drop . . . well, then I haven't got it no more, right?

AA. That's right.

XX. I work my ass off, but I get paid for it. And when I've gotten paid . . . I'll be rich . . . So it pays off . . . Right?

AA. It makes sense.

XX. Only, sometimes I wonder what's the use of it all?

AA. "All" what?

XX. Well, all I've got . . . I can't take it with me when I die. They won't let me get into paradise with it . . . and there's nothing I can do with it in hell. So why do I slave like this?

AA. It's you who wants it that way.

XX. Sure, but what do I get out of it? I'm ruining my health . . . And I don't have any pleasures. I don't drink . . . I don't smoke . . . except when you offer me one . . .

AA. (*offers him his package of cigarettes*) Go ahead, help yourself! Please!

XX. God bless you. (*He takes a cigarette, but then throws it back on the table.*) Tell me . . . what's the use. Eh? Why?

AA. What about your children? You're going to build

a house. You can leave that to your children when your time is up.

XX. And they, who're they going to leave it to?

AA. Their children.

XX. Ah . . . (*pause*) And how is it going to end?

AA. It doesn't end. Why d'you want it to end?

XX. Just like that, eh? . . . It doesn't end. You mean it'll never end?

AA. That's right — never.

XX. Hm . . . So you say there's no end . . . But how can that be seeing there was a beginning?

AA. You're asking some pretty difficult questions. Schopenhauer already wrestled with them.

XX. Who?

AA. Schopenhauer.

XX. A Jew?

AA. Not necessarily.

XX. Well, I don't like any of this. If there's a beginning there ought to be an end. If not, you can't have a beginning either . . . A hopeless beginning . . . And all this time I do nothing but slave and slave and slave. Never any pleasures . . . I never go to the cinema . . . I never go to any tarts . . . You think that's easy, do you?

AA. I never said it was.

XX. To bitch, like you, that's easy! But if you ever tried to live like me . . . (*He succumbs increasingly to self-pity.*) You know how I live? . . . Like an animal! Like a dog!

AA. No, you exaggerate a little.

XX. (*striking the table with his fist*) Don't you go contradicting me! Yes, like a dog! You said that yourself!

AA. If you remember, I was talking of an ox.

XX. (*bending close to AA, confidentially*) Come here. I'm going to tell you something.

AA. I'm listening.

XX. Closer . . . (*He puts his hands on AA's arms and pulls him closer to himself until their foreheads seem to touch. He whispers something with passion but discretely.*) And . . . and you were right. (*They return to their previous positions.*)

AA. (*with an exaggeratedly polite tone; upper-class*) But no, my dear boy . . .

XX. (*putting his index finger to his lips*) Hush! . . . (*He cries.*) Like a dog! . . . Dogs live better than I do. At least they don't have to work so hard . . . what sort of a life is this, eh? Tell me, you call that living?

AA. From a strictly biological point of view . . .

XX. Yes or no — is that what life is about?

AA. It depends.

XX. (*settling the question*) No. That's no kind of life . . . Pour us a drink!

AA. Perhaps we had enough for now.

XX. No, it's not enough! This is the first time I've had a drink since I came here. It's well deserved, don't you think?

AA. Without any doubt. (*AA refills the glasses. They drink.*)

XX. Ah, that feels good . . . I'm going to give you a riddle.

AA. Go ahead!

XX. Here it is: has, but has not.

AA. Wait a minute: "has . . ."

XX. . . . but has not. (*He laughs.*)

AA. "Has, but has not . . . Has, but has not . . ." — I have no idea.

XX. Guess!

AA. I can't. It's too difficult for me. (*XX strikes his chest with his fist.*) You? . . .

XX. Me.

AA. "Has . . ."

XX. . . . but has not! That's good, isn't it? (*He bursts out laughing.*)

AA. What is it that he "has"?

XX. (*stops laughing; in a menacing tone*) 'cause you don't think I have anything?

AA. Do you?

XX. You think I'm a have-not? My father was a have-not, my grandfather was a have-not, but not me! Okay, I'm gonna show you . . . (*He tries to get up, supporting himself heavily on the table.*)

AA. Never mind. It's not necessary. (*He puts his hands on XX's arms and pushes him down again. XX pulls away violently.*)

XX. I can afford it! Waiter! (*He makes a grand gesture across the table.*) This is my round.

AA. He is drunk . . . (*Pause. XX falls silent and lowers his head. AA inspects the bulb in the lamp.*) What's the matter with the light? (*Pause. XX gets up and staggers to the sink.*)

XX. Turn it on.

AA. It is turned on.

XX. Ah . . . (*Pause. XX is looking for the sink in the half-dark.*) What's turned on?

AA. The light.

XX. Aha . . . Now, if it's turned on, why are we in the dark?

AA. Because it's switched off. (*XX finally finds the sink. He puts his head under the tap and lets the water run.*) . . . Having said that, I ask myself why it is switched off. It should have come back on.

XX. (*his head still under the tap*) The New Year! The New Year!

AA. Yes, but it's taking a little too long.

THE EMIGRANTS

XX. Maybe it's the bulb . . . (*AA picks up the candle and climbs on a chair. He inspects the bulb, using the candle to give him light.*)

AA. No. The bulb is alright. (*He climbs down from the chair, goes to the door and opens it. He takes a quick look outside along the hall.*) Everybody is in the dark. Perhaps it's a short-circuit, or a power failure . . . (*He closes the door again and puts the candle back on the table.*) That's going to be the end of the candle.

XX. (*trying to parody him*) "that's going to be the end of the candle". . . . if you push down my cock like a handle.

AA. (*irritated*) Very funny . . .

XX. (*turns off the tap and dries his face vigorously with his hands*) You don't like that?

AA. No.

XX. Maybe you don't like me either.

AA. No.

XX. Well then what are you doing here, with me? (*pause*)

AA. That's a fundamental question.

XX. I didn't ask you to come here.

AA. True.

XX. You invited yourself. (*Pause. XX sits down, this time in the chair on the left of the table.*) Eh! Tell me, really, what in hell d'you want here with me?

AA. (*sitting down on the chair to the right*) Now? At this table?

XX. I'm not talking of the table. I want to know what you're doing here with me in this shitty place. (*AA shrugs his shoulders.*) What are you doing here?

AA. The same as you.

XX. That's not true. I have no choice. I'm a complete ox, an illiterate, an animal . . . But you, you've got an education, you speak foreign languages . . . You don't have to stay here.

AA. That's correct.

XX. You can make out anywhere. You can be successful anywhere—"Spic Ingliche" and all that . . . So what are you doing here? What are you looking for?

AA. Nothing.

XX. No, you're looking for something from me. Occasionally I ask myself questions: I am nothing to you, a stranger. You give me food to eat, you lend me money . . . You bitch about it, but you lend it to me . . . If you're not happy, what are you doing here with me? I'm not holding you back. Eh! What d'you want from me?

AA. Nothing.

XX. Don't treat me like an imbecile! I may be a brute, but I'm not an imbecile . . . You can tell me everything. After all, we're drinking together. Eh! Why are you drinking with me?

AA. To atone.

XX. Atone for what?

AA. For the sins of my forefathers. Our forefathers never drank together.

XX. Is that a sin?

AA. Yes, that's a sin. A national sin.

XX. You're pulling my leg.

AA. You don't believe me?

XX. No.

AA. You're right. You have the sound instinct of our people. In that case, I say to hell with our forefathers. Today, it's me, all alone . . . me . . . going to the people, fraternizing with the people, you understand? I am a "narodnik", a populist.

XX. A what?

AA. A "narodnik" . . . That's a nineteenth century

word. The idea too comes from the nineteenth century . . . It says that we must go back to the people, because our strength comes from the people . . .

XX. That's a lot of bullshit.

AA. Here we have the natural scepticism of the people. You have so many good qualities: a sound instinct, a sense of truth, the capacity for self-criticism . . . Well . . . I may be a philosopher, rationalist and progressive, but you — you are the locomotive of history, the vanguard of humanity. So what is so strange about my drinking with a locomotive? What is so surprising about my preparing a plate of fried eggs for the vanguard of humanity? That I walk in my drawers in the same room with it, and that I wipe my mouth with the same napkin as it? Have you ever thought of that? Eh?

XX. Bullshit.

AA. Alright. Let's forget about mystical sentiments of guilt and atonement for sins committed by past generations. Let's forget about nationalist dreams. Perhaps I am a socialist.

XX. Never.

AA. Why?

XX. Because I know socialists. We've got one that comes to the yard. Very polite. He never insults us. On the contrary. He's all smiles, he flatters us and brings us pamphlets, he explains things to us . . .

AA. I don't, eh?

XX. No.

AA. I suppose I insult you?

XX. And how! You're never content. This isn't right and that isn't right . . . And you keep on insulting me with your criticisms. One can see right away you're a gentleman, not a socialist.

AA. I see that one cannot fool you.

XX. That's for sure. I'm much too clever for that. I can see what's what right away. A socialist? I can smell them a mile away. But you, what could you possibly be, I mean seriously . . .

AA. Alright, what about a political agitator?

XX. Eh? . . . No, never. I'm small fry. The authorities aren't interested in me. It's the same here as in the old country. I'm good for nothing but hard work. If you were an agitator you wouldn't be staying here with me. You'd be somewhere else, with more important people — professors, people who think.

AA. Do you never think?

XX. Doesn't matter what I think . . . You want to know what I think? . . . I think of making money, of my children . . . of my good wife . . . Sometimes I think of tarts too. That's natural. Everybody thinks of that. The authorities aren't interested in that sort of thing. So long as I don't try to be a smart alec, so long as I stay quietly in my corner and do my work, the authorities don't care a damn what I think. They wouldn't bother sending an agitator here.

AA. Have you never thought about freedom?

XX. Meaning what?

AA. Well . . . to be free.

XX. How d'you mean?

AA. Well, for example, to say what you think.

XX. I already told you what I think. And I can repeat it for you. I can say it over and over from morning till night and from night till morning. Nobody stops me from saying what I think.

AA. But have you never thought about thinking any further?

XX. Think about thinking?

AA. You could put it like that . . .

XX. Certainly not. I'm not that stupid.

THE EMIGRANTS

AA. There is nothing stupid about thinking.

XX. That depends. Back home in my village, we had an idiot. He never did anything because he was no good at anything. He wasn't even good enough to look after the cows. He lived alone in a house, only from what people gave him. Well then, what was he doing when he did nothing? What was he thinking? What could he think about when he didn't know how to do anything and when he didn't do anything. He thought only about thinking, he thought about nothing else but his thoughts. And do you think he was intelligent? No, he was stupid . . . He was a lunatic.

AA. But he was free.

XX. Now I understand. You're a priest.

AA. A priest? Don't make me laugh.

XX. Yes. You're a priest of freedom. That's it. I should've known right away. When you shook me by the collar. A priest with his catechism! A priest who comes and says: beware of the power of the devil! Don't serve Satan! Serve Jesus Christ! But who is your Jesus Christ? Where is he? Show me? Is your God freedom? Then show me your freedom! Where is it? What is it? . . . I know only one kind of freedom — the freedom not to have to go to work. On Sundays, that's when I'm free. Give me seven Sundays a week and I shall kiss your feet as if you were Jesus himself. Seven Sundays — but paid!

AA. And if I were to take away from you even that single Sunday?

XX. You? What can you do? You can do nothing. You can give nothing and take nothing away from me. All you can do is lie on your divan and make up sermons. You're a divan apostle!

AA. You're right, I can't do anything. But the authorities can.

XX. Which means that one must be on the right side

of the authorities. Because if they can take things away, they can also give things. But you — you don't like the authorities, do you?

AA. I don't exactly dote on them.

XX. That's why they don't like you. And you want to know why you don't like them?

AA. I can't wait to find out.

XX. Because, before the authorities you're no better than me — with all your books and studies . . . You don't like that, eh? You think you're smarter than me when it comes to dealing with the authorities, don't you? . . . Well, when there's only one authority we're all equal, because we're all equally shit-scared! In a dictatorship we're all the same.

AA. Like in a public urinal.

XX. Why not? I'm not squeamish.

AA. Hear, hear! Come, let me embrace you.

XX. What for?

AA. Because you didn't let me down. I was right to count on you. I need precisely somebody like you. An ideal slave.

XX. And you don't think you're a priest?

AA. No. — Alright, I confess there were times when an evangelizing fancy took me. But that was before I understood . . . You don't have to be afraid that I'll try to convert you. The impulse has died. It was a passing foible, a momentary temptation. In fact, I'm not at all cut out to be a missionary. And besides, evangelizing is not my cup of tea.

XX. So you side with the authorities?

AA. Wrong again. No, I'm a very special case. I need a slave. Not for purposes of practical exploitation, of course. No. I need you as a model . . . You're indispensable to me as a landmark . . . Especially here.

XX. You're talking bullshit again.

AA. I'm not talking bullshit. You asked me to tell you who I really am and what I'm doing here with you. Now I'm going to tell you: I am the knight of the last chance — and do you know who my last chance is? You!

XX. I'm what?

AA. My only and my last chance . . . my muse . . . my inspiration . . .

XX. Hey, don't tell me you're homosexual.

AA. Listen. You are right, in a dictatorship all people are equal. Fear creates that equality. It took me a long time to reach that truth. And with what ease you made that discovery, with what simplicity you expressed such a fundamental fact! . . . I envy you. Sometimes simple humility is more insightful than intelligence.

XX. I told you before that I'm not as stupid as that.

AA. It leaves me speechless to see how a man, an intelligent man at that, like me, can refuse to see the most obvious truth when that truth hurts his pride. I behaved like a monkey in a cage. I swung back and forth from my tail, I took running leaps from the pole to the wire-fencing and back again to the pole, or when somebody threw me a nut I tried to get into the shell, all in order to feel the master of infinite spaces. It took me a long time to lose all my illusions, to reach an extremely simple conclusion: namely that I was a monkey in a cage.

XX. They're amusing, monkeys are. I've seen them in the zoo.

AA. You are right. Monkeys in a cage can be very amusing. When I finally realized that I was a monkey in a cage, I began to laugh at myself, and I laughed and laughed . . . till that laughter caught me by the throat and gave me the hiccups, till it turned into tears that drenched my monkey gob. That's when I realized that my antics weren't funny—except to the spectators and the keepers of the zoo: they never tired of throwing me nuts and candies, but the candies made me sick and I couldn't get inside the nutshells. That's how I learnt that there's no way out for a monkey—first of all, he has to admit that he is a monkey . . .

XX. Yes, yes, sure . . .

AA. Secondly, having established his condition as a monkey or a slave he must, without pride, derive at least some wisdom and some strength from it.

XX. From a monkey?

AA. Yes, my dear, from a monkey, from a monkey . . . Hasn't man descended from the monkey?

XX. No.

AA. That is your opinion. But science claims the contrary. Now, if man has descended from the monkey, then I, who am a monkey, am an aristocrat of humanity. It is in me as humiliated and caged monkey, in my condition of imprisonment, that all knowledge about man finds expression. A pure knowledge, a knowledge untouched as yet by the vicissitudes of evolution or the hazards of freedom. A primal knowledge. So I decided to take advantage of the opportunity, in other words, I, the caged monkey, decided to write a book about Man.

XX. A monkey can't write.

AA. Especially when he is in a cage. Exactly. But I didn't understand that until later. For the moment I was stunned by these new perspectives. I decided to write a book about Man in his pure state, that is to say about Man as a slave, that is to say about myself—the work of my life, unique of its kind, the first in the world. The excrement, the nutshells and all the other refuse which fouled up my cage suddenly turned into glittering diamonds. Such riches! I said to myself: we have nothing, but we do have our slavery. That's our treasure. What do others know about it? People here, for instance? They have written books about it, they've read all about it, but they haven't understood the essence of it. All literature about slavery is either dishonest or false. It's the work of either missionaries or liberators, or, at best, of free individuals or slaves who dream of freedom — that is to say, of slaves who are no longer entirely slaves. What do they know about the integrity of slavery, a self-sufficient state of being that doesn't seek transcendence? About a slavery that feeds on itself? What do they know about the joys and sorrows of slavery, its mysteries, beliefs and rituals? About the philosophy and cosmology of slavery, about its mathematics? They know nothing about it at all. But I, I know. So I decided to write about it.

XX. And have you written your book?

AA. No.

XX. Why not?

AA. Because I was afraid. (*pause*) Are you not going to ask me what I was afraid of? (*pause*) You're right. I'm talking to a compatriot . . . my Siamese twin . . . Anyway, the fact is that I was afraid, and that in order to write I had to stop being afraid. So, in order to escape fear I fled the country.

XX. And now, you're writing?

AA. No, not at the moment.

XX. Why not?

AA. Because I'm not afraid any more.

XX. You're never satisfied, so . . .

AA. It's a vicious circle. In order to take advantage of my only chance I lost it. In fleeing I stopped being a slave. I dissolved myself in freedom, scattered myself in it. I lost my subject, and what is worse, I lost the need for my subject . . . Theoretically, I still knew what I wanted, but I no longer had either the will or the need. And then, fortunately, I met you.

XX. What have I got to do with all that?

AA. Oh, you . . . You are exactly what I was when I ceased to exist. You are like a comet that fell on the earth and buried itself deeply in it. Immutable, unchanged, unaffected by your environment. A being from another world, a mineral from another planet. You, fortunately, are still a slave.

XX. I'm not going to sit here and let you call me names!

AA. But of course, of course you are a slave. And your vehement protest doesn't change anything. You are a heaven-sent, like a model, like an inspiration. I am reborn in you as a slave. You've restored to me my true self and my desire for self-determination. Thanks to you, I can at last write my great work. — Now do you understand why I need you?

XX. That's not the reason at all.

AA. Do you believe that I would stay here, of my own free will, with you, in this "shitty place", as you called it, — if I were not moved by a great project like that, imbued with a sense of mission?

XX. And I'm telling you that's not the reason.

AA. In that case, why am I here with you? Why, in your opinion? Come on, out with it — you tell me, if it's not asking too much.

XX. Because you like talking.

AA. I beg your pardon? What did you say?

XX. Yep. That's all. You like talking to me.

AA. And what could you and I talk to each other about?

XX. For instance, about flies. About flies and . . .

THE EMIGRANTS

and fly paper . . . of life back home, in the old country . . . Of the past . . . Just talk about it, remember the good old days . . . That's normal, isn't it? It's human, no? And who d'you want to talk to, if not to me? To them? (*He points to the ceiling.*)

AA. No!

XX. Of course not. What do they know about anything? But one fellow countryman always understands another. What are you trying to tell me with your stories about slaves? You simply want to talk, discuss things . . . It's normal . . . About summer and winter. About what we eat back home, what we drink . . . It's normal, no? . . . Among room-mates . . .

AA. It's not true! I have a great idea . . . a great project . . . a great work . . .

XX. Great work, my ass! . . . You think I don't see how you squirm when I receive a letter from home? You go to your corner and pretend to read a book — upside down! . . . I really feel sorry for you then . . . Because you never receive any mail.

AA. Because I don't need any . . .

XX. That's it . . . You don't receive any because nobody writes to you. You have nobody to write to, and nobody writes to you . . . You can talk, but write a book . . . You'll never write a book in your life, even if you know how to write . . . in several languages. Maybe it's just as well, because what would you want to write a book about, eh?

AA. About you.

XX. Come on. You'll just produce some sort of rubbish. And what good is that to anybody?

AA. I'll write for everybody.

XX. People have enough on their hands with their own rubbish; they don't need yours as well.

AA. People are always in need of the truth.

XX. Yes, but not any truth as disgusting as yours . . .

AA. Ah! You're afraid I'll write the shocking truth about you.

XX. You're going to write nothing.

AA. Why?

XX. Because you spend too much time lying on your divan.

AA. At the moment I'm organizing my thoughts, I'm studying, I'm weighing the pros and the cons . . .

XX. That's right . . . Always weighing things . . .

AA. But I'm going to start soon. Okay, why not tomorrow?

XX. Not tomorrow, nor the day after tomorrow . . . I know you well . . .

AA. In a year or two, then — what does it matter? It's important that the work is allowed to mature. Then it will bear fruit.

XX. You don't have that much time.

AA. We have all the time in the world. I shall stay with you for as long as it will take.

XX. Maybe you'll stay, but I won't.

AA. You are not going to move out . . . Who would pay the rent for you?

XX. Never mind, I'm moving back in.

AA. Where?

XX. Where d'you want me to go back to? Home, of course! I have somewhere to go back to, and I shall go back. But you, you'll stay here. Without me. Because you can't go back. You'll never go back. (*pause*) So? You still feeling smart-assed? Eh? (*pause*)

AA. When?

XX. Any time I want to. I'm going to stay here a little longer. I'm going to save a little more money and

THE EMIGRANTS

then — bjit! Goodbye! You won't see any more of me . . . I can go back home whenever I want.

AA. No, you can't. You'll never go back either.

XX. Me? Why not? . . . What's to stop me? I'm not a political refugee.

AA. At this time, you're not.

XX. I'm not afraid. They can't accuse me of anything.

AA. Are you sure?

XX. And what should I be afraid of? You have reason to be afraid. But I, I have nothing on my conscience.

AA. You say that I don't write letters. That's true. You say that I shall never write a book. Maybe. But there is something that I could write.

XX. And what is that?

AA. A denunciation. (*pause*)

XX. I have never done anything against our government.

AA. Is that so? And who associates with a traitor, a renegade, a degenerate, an enemy of the regime, that is to say — me? Eh? It wouldn't happen to be you, would it?

XX. No.

AA. What do you mean — "no"? You live with me, in the same room . . .

XX. Nobody knows.

AA. Are you sure? What if I were to write to the authorities? A few words are enough, even anonymously . . . You know how little it takes. And then — goodbye to your house, goodbye to your garden, goodbye to wife and children . . .

XX. Why?

AA. There you have it! You're still asking me why.

That's proof of your political depravity. It's not surprising, it's my influence . . . Tell me who you associate with and I tell you who you are . . . Have you already forgotten that it's enough to breathe the same air as a degenerate like me, to be contaminated yourself? And on top of that, you have talked to me, you have drunk with me . . . Who knows what you talked about . . . There was no witness. Do you think that when they gave you permission to go abroad, it was in order to associate with an anarchist?

XX. You're not going to do that to me!

AA. And why not?

XX. I've got a wife! And kids . . .

AA. Really? . . . Well, it was I who thought of them first. Yes, you have a wife and children, and that's why you will never go back to them. You wouldn't want to endanger their lives, would you? (*pause*) So, are you going to stay with me? (*pause*) Yes, you are staying, you're staying. I feel that you are going to stay. We are going to stay here together. You will send gifts to your children. For Christmas. They like that. As for your wife . . . Are you sure that she really needs you?

XX. No . . .

AA. You see, the pieces fit . . .

(*We hear the sound of a rapidly approaching siren.*)

XX. There's a fire.

AA. I hope it's not here. (*The sound of the siren is coming closer still.*)

XX. There's nothing burning here . . .

AA. No, but it's going to burn. Have you ever heard of Nero?

XX. No. Who's he?

AA. He was a Roman emperor. He burnt down his city because he was bored.

XX. (*suddenly interested*) He set fire to it?

AA. Of course. He could allow himself to do it because he was the only free man of his time. So you can imagine how bored he was. The whole freedom of the earth for a single human being, that's terrible. Not surprising that he wasn't able to resist doing it, the poor man . . . (*XX walks rapidly about the room, feeling the table and chairs with his fingers.*) And now, let's return to our own time. Here, in a democracy, everybody has a little freedom, less certainly than the emperor, but a good deal more than the emperor's subjects. So everybody is bored, in proportion to the amount of freedom he has. What is worse, everybody is bored with the boredom of the others who are bored . . . — What are you looking for?

XX. Nothing. Nothing.

AA. The sum total of boredom therefore always remains the same. Conversely, the risk of arson provoked by boredom increases in proportion to the number of free people. If, once upon a time, that risk stood at one chance in a million, it's a million in one today. In other words, fires are inevitable . . . — What are you doing?

XX. (*who has just brought his large suitcase out from under his bed, and who puts his pillow in his blanket*) I'm getting my bags ready.

AA. What for?

XX. Well, there's got to be a fire here, no?

AA. Not here! You don't understand. The fire starts on the upper floors where the free people live. Down here, there are only the emperor's subjects.

XX. That's the same thing.

AA. Not at all. It is not our fire. It's their fire.

XX. It's all the same.

AA. No! This is not an imperial fire. This is a democratic fire.

XX. If that's the way you want it . . .

AA. Let's not get mixed up in things that don't concern us. We have no right to this fire. At most we could go and sit out in the hall under the stairs and watch it from below, as befits slaves. The view from below has its advantages too. For instance, women run from fires. An opportunity you wouldn't want to miss! But beyond that, what does it have to do with us? It's neither our house nor our freedom. Come on, don't worry, leave your things alone. (*AA pours himself another cognac. Glass in hand, he walks across to the left of the stage and turns to face the proscenium with his profile to XX. XX deposits his suitcase, his bundle and the stuffed dog near the door and turns to AA.*) I drink to the health of all who don't have the right to immolate themselves and who must wait for the emperor to use his privilege. There they wait in silence and darkness, in the cold and in pain, for the Promethean magic to illumine and to warm them; they wait for the last fight, the sumptuous gift of the emperor. Yes, Gentlemen! Until we are illumined and warmed. Because nothing will illumine or warm us loyal subjects better than a fire prudently set. To our brothers!

(*He raises his glass. In the meantime the siren has reached its maximum intensity. XX extinguishes the candle. For a moment there is total darkness on stage. Abruptly, the bulb lights up, throwing a raw, violent light on the scene. On the floor above we hear a series of joyous exclamations, the 'aahs' of satisfaction and joy, as is normal in similar circum-*

THE EMIGRANTS

stances when the light reappears after a long period of darkness in a place where numerous persons have gathered. AA and XX find themselves face to face, AA is holding his glass in the air, XX is brandishing an axe. They remain motionless for several seconds. AA goes closer to XX and offers him his glass. XX lets his arm with the axe drop and accepts the glass.)

AA. (*continued*) They are gone.

XX. There's no fire.

AA. It wasn't necessarily a fire engine. It could have been the police, for example.

XX. You said there was a fire.

AA. An educated guess. It could also have been a strike.

XX. At the power station?

AA. At the water works or the power station. Maybe that's why there wasn't any water earlier. (*pause*) Did you intend to kill me? (*XX nods.*) I understand. You expected there would be a fire. And that the fire would burn up my corpse and destroy the evidence. I would have disappeared in the flames of a conflagration. Well, well . . . I must say, I underestimated you. (*He refills the second glass which stands on the table.*) But tell me, did you really believe everything I said about fires? Did you take me seriously? Did you believe this house was on fire?

XX. No.

AA. Well then? (*XX brings a box of matches from his pocket and throws it in the air several times. Then he puts the box back in his pocket.*) Ah! It's getting better and better. Not only murder but also arson. (*He raises his glass.*) To my health! (*They both drink.*) So then, if

I understood correctly, you believed that I ... — Do you still think me capable of writing that denunciation?

XX. Why not? (*He sits down on the chair to the left.*)

AA. Perhaps you're right. God alone knows what men are capable of. You can't be sure of anything. But I would not have written that denunciation. And not at all because I wouldn't know how; but quite simply because it would be superfluous. Since you are not going to go back. — Do you still need that axe? (*XX is silent.*) Even if you had killed me out of fear that I would denounce you, you still would not go back. So why should I bother to write that denunciation? Don't worry! I am not going to write it.

XX. No?

AA. No. Give me that. (*He gets up and takes the axe out of XX's hand. He goes to put it in a corner.*) You can thank heaven you failed. What would you do here, without me, all alone? ... Isn't it better that we stay together?

XX. I'm not going to stay here.

AA. But of course you're going to stay, even if you don't realize it yet.

XX. I want to go back.

AA. Sure you do. I believe you. You are here precisely because you want to go back. Your return home is your sole *raison d'être*. Without that, you wouldn't stay here another minute, you'd go mad ... or you'd kill yourself.

XX. So who's going to stop me leaving?

AA. (*turning to the right, to where XX has left his bags and the dog PLUTO*) Pluto! Here, Pluto! ... How stubborn that dog is! (*He heads for the door and picks up the dog.*)

XX. (*getting up*) Leave that alone!

AA. I'm not going to murder it . . . You see, little doggie – this gentleman is jealous. Your master is jealous of you. He never lets me play with you . . . Such a deep attachment to a dog isn't normal. To a plush dog at that.

XX. Put it down!

AA. Why? Don't I have a right to caress it? Why are you always so jealous of this dog? That's odd. It's strange. It's suspicious.

XX. I'm not jealous at all. (*He sits down again.*)

AA. Ah! How well you look after him! . . . It looks as if he were going to burst – he's so fat. What do you give him to eat?

XX. Nothing. He is stuffed.

AA. Yes, of course. But with what? What is there inside him?

XX. There's nothing.

AA. Maybe it's a secret.

XX. (*gets up*) Are you going to leave it alone or not?

AA. Let's get to the bottom of this! (*He picks up the scissors from the floor and before XX can stop him he cuts open the stomach of the plush dog: out tumble bundles of banknotes.*) Ah! – so that's it! Now I understand.

XX. It belongs to me! Give it back to me! (*He grabs the money from him.*)

AA. I understand everything. That's why you never have any money.

XX. Give it back to me, you thief!

AA. Watch what you say. If I had wanted to rob you, I could have done so a long time ago. You think I never saw you put away that money?

XX. You were spying on me, eh?

AA. At first, it was only a matter of suspicion. People

like you don't keep their money in the bank. And then, one evening . . .

XX. You saw me.

AA. Yes. I saw how you stuffed your dog with banknotes. It happened quite unintentionally, I assure you. But we intellectuals are light sleepers.

XX. Thief! (*He sits at the table, on the chair on the right, and begins to count his money.*)

AA. You can check . . . I haven't taken a penny. Mind you, I could have . . . And I even had a right to . . .

XX. What right? It belongs to me!

AA. You owe me quite a lot of money . . .

XX. It's not for me . . .

AA. I know. I know. It's for your wife and children. But what do I care who you are saving your money for? What matters to me is that you are a miser. For me that's the best guarantee that you will never leave me. Because you'll never let go of your money—isn't that right?

XX. You think I'm going to leave it to you? You can wait a long time . . .

AA. I've never thought that. I'm not even going to ask you to pay me back your debts.—So, you propose to take it back home with you, do you?

XX. It belongs to me! It's mine! I'm not giving it to anyone.

AA. You have no idea how I love to hear you say "me" and "my" and "mine" . . . You pronounce these words with such conviction, such passion. But have you considered that over there you'd have to spend all this money which it has taken you so much trouble to amass? Back home you can neither make money nor save any . . .

XX. That's exactly why I've been saving up over here.

AA. That's it — "here"! Over here and not over there
... Here you save a little more money every day, you lie on your bed thinking how tomorrow you'll have a little more money, the day after still more, and in a year's time lots and lots more. You have a goal in life that grows more seductive the further removed it is. Have you already saved enough for a little house with a little garden? So, why not try to save some more until you can afford a bigger house with a bigger garden? It's quite simple. All you have to do is to postpone your return for a month or two. And then, why not an even bigger house with an even bigger garden? ... And so you keep on postponing your return because the more money you have the more you want to have. The years pass and you're forever setting a new date for your return home, forever working and saving — for later on!
... Hey, you've stopped. Why? It's so pleasant to watch you count your money ...

XX. Why are you telling me all this?

AA. So that you understand that it isn't me who is holding you back. It isn't necessary for me to write a letter of denunciation to make you stay ... You are going to stay here of your own free will. That's why I'm telling you all this. And also to make sure you don't take it into your head to play with an axe again.

XX. I'm not going to go back home?

AA. Never. Even though you'll always be under the impression that it's just a matter of days, that soon ...

XX. Never?

AA. Why make so much of it? You have a good life, full of hope, nostalgia and illusions. Not everybody is so lucky.

XX. But why "never"?

AA. I've already told you. Because you are a slave.

Over there you're a slave of the State. Here you're a slave of your own greed. Whatever happens, you'll always be a slave. There's no possible liberation for you. Freedom means to be master of oneself. But in your case there's always someone else or something else, that is your master. If it's not people, it's things.

XX. What things?

AA. The things you want to own, possess — things you can buy with your money. To be a slave of things is a form of slavery much more perfect than the best slavery you can get in prison. A truly ideal slavery — because there are no external restraints, not a single restriction. Your slavery is solely the creation of a slavish spirit thirsting for slavery. You have the soul of a slave, and that's why you interest me, on account of my work about the nature of slavery, a work I have every intention of writing . . .

XX. You know where you can stick your work . . .

AA. I couldn't care less what you think about my research. A scientist pays no attention to what the insect thinks of the microscope. I observe you, and I describe you — that's all.

XX. Who? Me?

AA. Yes, you. And what you think of that is of no importance at all. The only thing that matters is that you cannot stop being a slave any more than an insect can stop being an insect.

XX. Can't I?

AA. No, you can't. Because you can't change your nature. You can't because you would have to become someone else . . . and that's impossible. You can't because you can't stop being a son of a bitch, any more than you can stop dreaming of your return home, any more than you can help the fact that you never will . . . go back.

XX. I'll go back home.

AA. You won't.

XX. I will!

AA. And what about that? (*He points to the bundles of money.*)

XX. I'll go back! I'll go back! I'll go back! (*Each time he bangs the table with his fist. Then, suddenly, he begins to tear up the banknotes.*)

AA. What on earth are you doing?! That's your money!

XX. I'm a slave! . . . I'm an insect! . . . (*AA tries to stop him, but XX pushes him away. He tears the bills into little pieces which he scatters all around himself.*)

AA. That's your money!

XX. My money . . . my hard-earned pennies . . . my savings . . . It's mine . . . mine! (*He goes on tearing up his money. AA tries to subdue him, but XX pushes him away so violently that AA staggers, stumbles, and falls to the ground. XX completes his work of destruction.*)

AA. You've gone mad. (*Moving on all fours, he picks up the torn bills from the floor.*) Maybe one can stick them together again . . .

XX. You think so?

AA. No. (*throws the money on the floor and gets up*)

XX. Now what am I going to do?

AA. How do I know? . . . You can do what you like . . . You are a free man now.

XX. What in hell came over me?

AA. Why are you complaining? You have delivered yourself from the condition of slavery, you have rebelled against the tyranny of money. You have proven that you can afford the luxury of freedom. You should be happy . . .

XX. But now I won't be able to go back home.

AA. You couldn't have gone back before, either. So, what's the difference?

XX. It's all your fault.

AA. Did I ask you to tear up your money? All I did was to indulge in theoretical speculations, but you — you had to go and play Spartacus . . .

XX. Me? I didn't want anything! All I wanted was to go back home . . . that's all.

AA. Too late. (*He fetches his suitcase from under his bed and gets out several sheets of manuscript. He sits down at the table on the chair to the left. He begins to tear up the pages methodically.*)

XX. What's that?

AA. Plans, outlines, sketches, drafts. I was going to write a great work.

XX. So, why are you tearing it all up?

AA. Because I am no longer going to write it. I have come to realize that the ideal slave doesn't exist, since even a convict like you has his moment of freedom . . . You were a model for me, an inspiration, a thesis and a certainty. In one instant you have destroyed the fruit of my experiences and my reflections. You have nipped a great work in the bud. You're nothing but a vandal, a hooligan —

XX. Hey . . . shut your fucking mouth!

AA. Well, of course you don't give a damn! Because of this act of yours, this one stupid act, humanity has suffered an irreparable loss — and you don't give a damn! My work was going to make an important contribution to world culture . . . But of course, what is that to you?

THE EMIGRANTS

... One of the most original contributions! ... And you don't give a damn!

XX. (*Gets up and takes off his jacket which he hangs over the back of the chair. He climbs up on the chair and then on to the table.*) Move over.

AA. To think that you were such a fine slave! ... You have ruined everything. You think only of yourself. (*XX takes off his tie and makes a noose of it. This he attaches to the electric wire near the socket with the naked bulb.*) Are you going to hang yourself?

XX. Don't tell me I haven't got the right to do it.

AA. Of course you do ... You have every right. Suicide is the supreme right of the free man, the ultimate affirmation of freedom.

XX. So, move!

AA. (*moving the papers to the edge of the table.*) In fact, it would be the logical consequence of your previous action. Since you have begun to be free, one can't refuse you anything anymore. Although, I should warn you, it's better not to go overboard ...

XX. (*pulling the tie to test its strength*) That should hold ...

AA. Excess and exaggeration are in bad taste. But bad taste is a characteristic trait of all people of the lowest social classes. Say, you wouldn't consider dropping it, would you?

XX. (*putting his head through the noose*) Move!

AA. Why?

XX. Because I'm going to kick away the table.

AA. If you insist ... That's what I call the greed of the opportunist.

XX. I told you to get out of the way.

AA. Rude and stubborn ...

XX. Are you going to goddam move or not?

AA. Do you really have to be so vulgar? Don't blaspheme!

XX. Okay. I'm still going to kick that table.

AA. Wait! What is your last word?

XX. You can go and f- . . .

AA. Hold it! Don't go on! Leave me with the memory of a man with a refined soul, even though of common origin . . . I know what you wanted to say, but that was intended for me. Now what about your family?

XX. My family?

AA. Have you forgotten that you have a family? After all, you owe them a few words. (*pause*)

XX. They can't hear me.

AA. Write to them!

XX. Now?

AA. Sure, right now! You are going to hang yourself, so you won't have another opportunity.

XX. It's too late.

AA. I'll write for you. All you have to do is dictate. Come on! Move over! (*He takes the last sheet of paper, which is not yet torn up, and turns the blank side up. He gets his pen out of his pocket.*) Okay, go ahead!

XX. My dear wife, my dear children . . .

AA. (*writes mouthing the words*) . . . my . . . dear . . . children —

XX. I'm writing to let you know that I'm in good health . . .

AA. . . . in . . . good . . . health . . . Hm! . . . Well, let's go on. (*He writes.*) What's next?

XX. I hope you are doing as well as I . . .

AA. Maybe you'd better not say that.

XX. Why?

AA. It's not quite the thing to say. (*He moves his*

THE EMIGRANTS

forefinger across his throat and sticks out his tongue.) It's true . . . but you'd better not . . . (*AA reading it back:*) " . . . to let you know that I'm in good health." Period. What's next?

XX. . . . and that I am doing quite well.

AA. (*writing*) In heaven . . .

XX. (*who goes on mechanically*) As on earth . . . (*He corrects himself.*) Why "in heaven"?

AA. Surely you'll go to heaven . . .

XX. That's none of your business. Cross that out!

AA. Alright. Next?

XX. I don't know.

AA. You want me to write on your behalf?

XX. Go ahead! Write!

AA. (*writing*) I-miss-you-and-the-children . . .

XX. Good.

AA. And that's why I want to hang myself.

XX. What?

AA. Hang myself.

XX. No, not that. Don't write that . . .

AA. But it's the truth.

XX. That's got nothing to do with it.

AA. Okay. (*He writes.*) . . . I'm going to hang myself because I don't miss you at all.

XX. No!

AA. You mean you don't like that either?

XX. Not like that! . . . What kind of an intellectual are you who can't even write a letter!

AA. So, go ahead! . . . How would you phrase it?

XX. I don't know . . . I'd make it shorter.

AA. I'm going to hang myself. With all my love. Your father and husband. — Sign! (*He holds out to XX the sheet of paper and his pen. XX skims the text, crumples up the paper and throws it on the floor. He takes his head out of the noose and comes down from the table.)* So, you don't want to write anymore? (*XX turns his back to walk over to the right.)* Hey! My pen! (*XX gives him the pen and lies down on his bed, on the right, turning his face to the wall.)* As you like. (*He climbs on the table and removes the tie from the lamp. He throws the tie on the chair to the right.)* You are right, not everything is lost. I'm not talking of myself, but of you. You can start from scratch.

(*Up above, we hear a door slam, people going downstairs, laughter, voices.*)

AA. (*continued*) You'll see how happy your wife will be. And your children? They're waiting for you. They're expecting you. Your wife is waiting for you too . . . She longs for you to return . . . Imagine the explosion of joy! Everybody will turn out to welcome you, the whole village! Who knows, perhaps there'll even be a band. (*A last burst of laughter on the stairs. Silence. XX doesn't reply.*) And the presents, just think of the presents! By god! All the nice things you'll be bringing them. A present for everybody. And you know exactly the right thing to bring to each one. You'll buy to your heart's content. Whole suitcases full of all kinds of nice things. How jealous people will be! I can see it from here. (*XX doesn't reply.*) Everyone will envy you, you'll see. (*He goes to the right where XX has left his things, picks up a blanket and covers XX with it. He goes to the left and lies down on his bed, on his back with his hands under his head.*) And then, you're going to build a house. A beautiful house. Large, and made of freestone. Not some kind of shack. And you'll have your flies too . . . (*pause*) You'll send your kids to school . . . Give them an education, let them go places! Give them a chance to be somebody! It'll be a good school, a real school . . . And then everything will be good and true . . . Work will provide bread, and the law freedom, because freedom will be the law and the law will be freedom! Isn't that what we are looking for? What we are all aiming for? And if we all have a common goal, if we all want the same thing, what prevents us from creating a community, a healthy community, wise . . . You'll go back home and you'll never again be a slave. Neither you, nor your children . . .

(*XX starts to snore very noisily. AA turns on his side to face the wall. After a while another sound is heard over the snoring of XX, a sound that begins quietly and gradually becomes louder: sobs, poignant, heart-rending sobs!*)

THE END

MUSIC USE NOTE

Licensees are solely responsible for obtaining formal written permission from copyright owners to use copyrighted music in the performance of this play and are strongly cautioned to do so. If no such permission is obtained by the licensee, then the licensee must use only original music that the licensee owns and controls. Licensees are solely responsible and liable for all music clearances and shall indemnify the copyright owners of the play(s) and their licensing agent, Samuel French, against any costs, expenses, losses and liabilities arising from the use of music by licensees. Please contact the appropriate music licensing authority in your territory for the rights to any incidental music.

IMPORTANT BILLING AND CREDIT REQUIREMENTS

If you have obtained performance rights to this title, please refer to your licensing agreement for important billing and credit requirements.